IRISH LAW AND LAWYERS IN
MODERN FOLK TRADITION

* Volumes 1–7 are published by Irish Academic Press.

Irish Law and Lawyers in Modern Folk Tradition

ÉANNA HICKEY

FOUR COURTS PRESS
in association with
THE IRISH LEGAL HISTORY SOCIETY

Typeset in 11 pt on 14 pt Plantin by
Carrigboy Typesetting Services, County Cork for
FOUR COURTS PRESS LTD
Fumbally Court, Fumbally Lane, Dublin 8, Ireland
e-mail: info@four-courts-press.ie
and in North America for
FOUR COURTS PRESS
c/o ISBS, 5804 N.E. Hassalo Street, Portland, OR 97213.

A catalogue record for this title is available
from the British Library.

ISBN 1–85182–460–X

Printed in Great Britain by
MPG Books, Bodmin, Cornwall

To my father, Michael, and to my children

Contents

List of illustrations

With the exception of illustration 9 (see pp. 179–80) the illustrations appear between pages 112 and 113.

Abbreviations

Amer Hist Rev	*American Historical Review*
Cox CC	Cox's Criminal Cases
IFC	Irish Folklore Collection
IHS	*Irish Historical Studies*
ILT & SJ	*Irish Law Times & Solicitor's Journal*
ILTR	Irish Law Times Reports
IR	Irish Reports
IR CL	Irish Reports, Common Law series
Ir Eq	Irish Reports, Equity series
Ir Jur	*Irish Jurist*
Louth Arch Soc Jn	*Journal of the County Louth Archaeological Society*
LQR	*Law Quarterly Review*
LR Ir	Law Reports, Ireland
NI	Northern Ireland Law Reports

Preface

I HAVE A GOOD FRIEND who entered college at the same time
as I did. We chose separate paths – law and history. In our third
year, however, we were brought together for the study of legal
history – an interdisciplinary subject. It was a revelation to me how
much we differed in our approach to the material. Our focus, our
analyses, the approaches we took were fundamentally different. It
was then I realised that, for better or worse, I was a lawyer. All the
time I was at university, I had supposed my task to be that of
learning the Law; in fact, I was absorbing a way of thinking: a set
of intellectual tools and values to be applied to resolving any legal
problems I might encounter in the future.

To me, the primary hallmark of the legal mind is a drive towards
precision in speech and thought. While it is true that if there were
no ambiguous laws there would be no lawyers, the essential goal
of the lawyer is nonetheless to replace ambiguity with certainty.
Owing to the complexity of society, the remarkable ingenuity of
mankind, and the limited capacity of language to describe the
world as it really is, that goal is never reached. But I think that to
be a lawyer is to operate, consciously or unconsciously, on the
premise that this goal is worth striving for. The struggle to make
and interpret laws is rooted in a deeper philosophical battle: the
desire of men and women to say what we mean, and to be understood.

Having begun to recognise the attributes of my own particular
training, I began to wonder what it would be like to apply that
training to matters outside of the normal legal purview. That was
when I was introduced to folklore, and the idea for this book
started to take shape.

The particular characteristics of the oral folk tradition as an
historical source will be dealt with in detail in the opening chapter,
along with the other sources upon which I rely during the course

of this book. For the moment, I will simply say that as a lawyer, I found it initially hard to come to terms with the fluidity of the oral tradition. When one is used to the authoritative language in which statutes or written judgments are expressed, it is dizzying to discover that an eminently believable folk story, told with a similar air of authority, and containing a wealth of names and local detail, is in fact no more than a version of an archetypal tale, to be found across the country (and possibly the world). Law stresses the primacy of the written word. The basic rule of legal interpretation, from a humble business contract to the Constitution of Ireland, is that words are taken at face value. What was said is presumed to be what was meant. In a folk narrative, it is assumed that the words spoken are unreliable to a greater or lesser extent, and the true meaning of a story is often found in what was not said. Once I accepted this, it became clear that folklore had some interesting things to say about law; and that the folklore of law could tell us some interesting things about Irish people.

One more preliminary point needs to be made concerning the folk sources that I have referred to in this book. These stories, proverbs, songs and opinions come largely from the archives of the Irish Folklore Commission (about which I shall have more to say in the first chapter). As it happened, many of the narratives relating to law were in English; the remainder were in Irish, with spellings varying according to regional custom and pronunciation. No doubt, there are also some spelling mistakes made by the collectors who wrote them out.

Originally, I thought it better, when quoting from the archives, to do so verbatim, without corrections of any kind. My feeling was that to correct these passages would, in some way, detract from their character. I also felt that the language used could tell us some interesting things about Irish culture – things which are, admittedly, beyond the scope of this book – such as, for instance, the encroachment of anglicised words and spellings on the Irish language. However, it is the policy of the Department of Irish Folklore at University College Dublin (who are guardians of the folklore archives) that all quotations in Irish be 'standardised'. This means that while idioms and regional phrases are left untouched, spelling and grammar have been adjusted to conform with the accepted modern standard.

All quotations in English can be taken to have been in English originally, and are unaltered. I have supplied translations of any Irish passages, and have occasionally suggested interpretations for unclear or slang phrases in either tongue. Finally, it will be noted that in my discussion of folk narratives I tend to use words such as 'allegedly' and 'apparently', as an occasional reminder of their doubtful historicity. This does not mean that where such words are not used, I believe the story to be true. But what I have come to understand is that, for the most part, the issue of truth or falsehood is largely irrelevant to what can be learned from these narratives. We are not now in court, but in the realm of social history, and to focus constantly on superficial lies and errors would be to miss the underlying truths and belief-patterns which may tell us more about ourselves as a people than all the law reports in all the libraries of Ireland.

I am grateful to the Department of Irish Folklore, University College Dublin for permission to use extracts from their folklore collection. They also possess a remarkable assembly of travel guides and tourist books from down the centuries which were equally invaluable to me. Professor Séamas Ó Catháin and all his staff were unfailingly kind and helpful, but I owe an especial debt of thanks to Críostóir Mac Carthaigh and Bairbre Ní Fhloinn, who helped me in many ways, not least with the standardisation of quotations in Irish. My thanks also to Professor W.N. Osborough, who first planted the seeds of this project in my head, and whose knowledge, enthusiasm and effort have contributed greatly to it. I must thank the photographic department of the National Library for permission to use certain illustrations; and the Ulster Folk and Transport Museum for permission to reproduce an extract from *Ulster Folklife*. I am also in debt to the Chief Justice of Ireland, Mr Justice Liam Hamilton, and to Mrs Justice Susan Denham for allowing me the space and time to continue my research and writing during these last three years.

Finally, on a personal note, I wish to thank my family, and especially my wife Carole, for their encouragement and support.

CHAPTER ONE

Introduction to the sources

The historian is like someone whose only way of viewing a landscape is by looking at photographs. He can see everything that is revealed by the photograph, but has no idea what exists beyond the field of vision covered by the camera.... Every photograph of the past has been made with a special kind of camera, fitted with a lens that is suitable for a given situation. Each type of historical source not only has its own limitations, but also its own particular way of seeing things – its own particular bias.... Comparison of oral sources with other kinds of historical sources is a little like juxtaposing and superimposing a number of photographs one with and upon the other, so that a larger area of the landscape can be seen, and seen more clearly.[1]

THIS BOOK IS CONCERNED with what can be learned of popular attitudes to law, lawyers and the legal system in Ireland over the last 250 years or so, from folk, literary and other materials. The primary sources are written records of oral traditions – coming in the main from the archives of the Department of Irish Folklore (formerly the Irish Folklore Commission)[2] at University College Dublin – supplemented with facts, stories and opinions gathered from such disparate sources as historical treatises, articles on folklore, diaries of travellers in Ireland over the period in question, and works of fiction recognised as having strong folkloric overtones. None of these sources are overly familiar to the lawyer or the historian, and so I feel I must preface my work with a few remarks on the origin, nature, benefits and dangers of each. I begin with folklore.

FOLKLORE

The vast bulk of the folklore material comes, as I have indicated, from the archives of the Irish Folklore Commission. This body

---

1   Jan Vansina, *Oral tradition* (London, 1965), p. 141.
2   The initials IFC now refer to the Irish Folklore Collection.

was established in 1935, to collate, preserve, analyse and dissemi-
nate Irish folklore in all its many forms. Full-time and part-time
collectors worked for years with industry and passion, gathering
the leavings of a receding cultural tide. They recorded songs, stories,
recipes, anecdotes, poems and customs from all over the country.
Their work forms the backbone of the manuscript collection
currently housed in the Department of Irish Folklore at University
College Dublin. It is supplemented by a special schools collection
– undertaken as a national project between 1936 and 1938, with
the help of teachers, pupils and parents of primary schools across
Ireland.

One of the founding fathers of folklore research in Ireland was
Seán Ó Súilleabháin. In 1942, in order to assist both professional
and amateur collectors in their work, he published a *Handbook of
Irish folklore*. In it, he sought to highlight areas of folk life, custom
and belief which might profitably be explored by collectors. For
each subject, he provided a series of sub-headings, along with
samples of questions which he believed would elicit the most
useful information. Guidelines as to the form in which folklore
should be recorded were included, as were a number of salutary
warnings on the necessity to record information accurately, completely, and contemporaneously where possible.

The importance of Ó Súilleabháin's handbook cannot be over-
emphasised. To this day, it is the basis on which the manuscript
and schools collections are indexed. In its practicality, breadth of
vision, and ability to fire the imagination of collectors and enthu-
siasts, it remains unique. The years of research which have culminated in the present book began with my being told that, within
the *Handbook*, there was a section on law and legal administration.[3]
Not having any idea of how much material there might be, but
intrigued by the possibility of discovering a whole new approach
to law, I was drawn to find out what was there. As shall become
clear, I found a great deal.

Folklore is perhaps the most maligned and misunderstood of
academic disciplines; the poor relation of 'proper' history, 'proper'
literary studies, or 'proper' anthropology. In the introduction to

---

3 Seán Ó Súilleabháin, *A handbook of Irish folklore* (Dublin, 1942), pp. 164–70.

his book, *Folklore and fakelore*, Richard Dorson complained, 'No subject of study in the United States today is more misunderstood than folklore. I can make this statement with some confidence, for my academic life has been largely spent in attempts to combat these misunderstandings.'[4] Advocates of folklore research have never been reticent about the shortcomings and limitations of oral traditions as a source of objective historical truth, and these are indeed substantial. There are many chaotic elements at work, stirring up mud where once was pristine historical clarity; rendering it impossible to speak of certainties, and sometimes withdrawing even probabilities; leaving only informed speculation as to the true picture. The principal problems may be identified as concerning (i) historical trustworthiness; (ii) regional variation; and (iii) scarcity of evidence.

SHORTCOMINGS OF ORAL TRADITION

Historical trustworthiness

It is important to realise that folklore and folk traditions serve particular purposes within the communities from which they emerge. Those purposes are unlikely to include a desire to preserve all the facts surrounding an event for posterity. Detailed historical accuracy is rarely a primary aim of the storyteller, and often may not feature at all. Paramount in most storytellers' minds is that they tell a good story; and what makes a good story is not necessarily the truth – an axiom well known to today's tabloid newspapers. Even where they are attempting to stick to the literal truth, there are many subliminal factors influencing these amateur historians; factors of which they may well remain unaware, and which they are accordingly unable to counteract. These include: the psychological make-up of the informant; the cultural and social values impinging upon him or her; the defence of private or community interests; the storyteller's relationship with the person who eventually records the story as a piece of folklore; questions from the interviewer that indicate what kind of answer he or she expects or desires; the age of the informant; and

4   Richard Dorson, *Folklore and fakelore* (Cambridge, Mass., 1976), p. 1.

his or her motives behind telling the story. These factors operate not only on the person who tells the story to the folklore collector, but on every link in the storytelling chain since the story was first told. Again, similar factors may operate on the folklore collector who finally records the account, in inverse proportion to his or her skill as a field researcher. To borrow a maxim from quantum mechanics: the act of observation affects the thing observed.

Regional variation

There is another factor which affects the historical trustworthiness of folk tales. It is well known to students of folklore that variants of the same folk tale can be found in places as far apart as Ireland and India. Antti Aarne (1867–1925) was a pioneer in attempting to categorise folk tales according to a list of archetypal stories and characters. His *Verzeichnis Märchentypen*, published in 1910, was revised and expanded by Stith Thompson in 1928 under the title *Types of the folktale in world literature*. In 1955, Thompson undertook a large-scale revision of this work. This edition, published under the title *Motif-index of folk literature*, has become the cornerstone of folklore scholarship in Europe and beyond. Reference to this work shows us that in many cases, what purports to be an account of real historical events is in fact an instance of a common motif in international folk literature, with people and place-names inserted to give a local flavour. An example which shall be referred to in a later chapter is the so-called 'trespasser's defense', in which a man places earth from his own land in his shoes, so that no matter where he walks, he is standing on his land.[5] As well as the internationally known tales, there can arise regional archetypes peculiar to Ireland. For instance: accounts of a person having the power to save someone from hanging are found in different parts of the country. The identity of the person and other details concerning the extent and origin of the power may differ, but the basic story remains the same.[6] With stories or people that capture the public's imagination in a powerful way,

---

5   Stith Thompson, *Motif-index of folk literature* (Bloomington, Indiana, 1955), J 1161.3. An Irish variant of this tale is mentioned in chapter 5 below, at p. 94.
6   See below, pp. 48–50.

this is especially common. Ríonach Uí Ógáin, in her study of the folklore surrounding Daniel O'Connell, identifies numerous tales which are classifiable under the Aarne-Thompson index, and a number of others which form archetypes peculiar to Ireland – for instance, the 'anam sa chorp' tale.[7]

Chronological accuracy

The stories and accounts in the archives of the Department of Irish Folklore cover a period of approximately 300 years, and it can be extremely difficult to place events accurately within this timespan. Apart from events which can be dated from more mainstream historical sources – such as the infamous 'Wildgoose Lodge' murders (30 October 1816), which form the topic of three articles in the *Journal of the County Louth Archaeological Society*[8] – most folk narratives are told without any particular concern as to when the events described occurred. Where dates are given, they are invariably approximate ('In my father's time', 'When I was young', 'In the olden days'), and cannot be trusted. A good example is a phrase that crops up frequently and in relation to a number of topics: 'Fifty years ago'. This is usually no more than a euphemism for 'a long time ago' – the storyteller plucking a date out of the air to lend credence to the historicity of his or her tale.

Meaningful comparison between stories is rendered difficult by this imprecision: similar narratives may in fact relate to separate generations. The man who says 'people were fond of going to law' and the man who disagrees may be concerned with entirely different periods of history. Tales and stories sometimes have within them broad clues as to their origin; but references to people, places or events which can be dated may be misleading. Consider a story from Cavan of two people arrested for drunkenness, one a Protestant, the other a Catholic. The storyteller said that the

---

7   'Life in the body' – see below, p. 78. Also Ríonach Uí Ógáin, *Immortal Dan* (Dublin, 1995), and its earlier Irish version, *An rí gan choróin* (Dublin, 1984).
8   T.F.G. Paterson, 'The burning of Wildgoose Lodge', *Louth Arch Soc Jn*, xii (1950), 159; D.J. Casey, 'Wildgoose Lodge: the evidence and the lore', *Louth Arch Soc Jn*, xviii (1956), 140; Réamonn Ó Muirí, 'The burning of Wildgoose Lodge: a selection of documents', *Louth Arch Soc Jn*, xxi (1986), 117.

Catholic was given a month's hard labour, whereas Flanagan, the Protestant, was released with a fine of half a crown. He added that Joseph Biggar raised the issue of these bigoted judgements in Parliament, and his lobbying resulted in the introduction of Catholic magistrates into Ireland.[9] The connection with Biggar would seem to place the events of the story towards the end of the nineteenth century; but we know in fact that Catholic magistrates existed fully 40 years before Biggar's stint as an MP. The dating of the story becomes impossible without further knowledge – was Biggar actually involved with the case or was it someone else? Is some, or indeed any of this story true? We cannot say. Our inability to date anything other than approximately also affects analysis of proverbs and sayings. When were they first popularised? How long did they remain in use? One can only speculate.

Scarcity of evidence

All history is necessarily incomplete; but this is especially true of folk history. One could flood the world with folklore collectors, armed to the teeth with dictaphones, shorthand pads and laptop computers, and still the hopes, dreams, views and stories of the vast bulk of humanity would remain hidden from academic eyes. As the poet says:

Unrecorded, unrenowned,
Men from whom my ways begin,
Here I know you by your ground
But I know you not within –
There is silence, there survives
Not a moment of your lives.[10]

How then can it be said with any degree of certainty that those opinions and beliefs which have been recorded represent the opinions and beliefs of the unrecorded majority? In the course of my researches into the folklore of law in Ireland I have found little

---

9 Irish Folklore Collection (IFC) Ms. Vol. 1196, p. 165. Joseph Gillis Biggar (1828–90), born in Belfast; MP for Co. Cavan 1874–90.
10 E. Blunden, 'Forefathers' in *The new Oxford book of English verse* (Oxford, 1972), p. 907.

exact repetition of views or stories, and what source material there is does not derive evenly from all parts of the country. Naturally, the diligence and breadth of interest of collectors vary considerably: so while the archives contain much material of value from Ulster and Munster (in particular the counties of Cavan and Kerry), there is comparatively little from Connacht, and virtually nothing from Leinster, where the oral tradition has been longest under threat. All this combines to weaken the persuasive force of generalised statements and hypotheses drawn from folk sources. Mainstream history deals mostly with named individuals, each with their own personal history which is taken into account when their impact on the broader social and historical canvas is being measured. Folklore, by its very nature, is more anonymous. Stories, sayings and beliefs are passed orally from one generation to another, acquiring a near-timeless core, over which each retelling lays a thin veil of contemporaneity. The names and lives of most of those in the storytelling chain remain forever obscured. It is tempting, therefore, to regard 'the Folk' as a kind of homogeneous mass with one mind; one set of values, customs and opinions. Reality, of course, is never so obliging. Just as the famous judicial figure of the Man on the Clapham Omnibus does not exist, so too there is no archetypal Rural Irish Peasant from whom all of the common people of Ireland were cloned. It is important to bear this in mind when examining what purport to be popular sayings and opinions; while folklore can point towards the existence of communal beliefs and attitudes, we must remember that the full picture eludes us, and always will.

So then, with formidable drawbacks attaching to the study of folklore as an historical discipline, what, if any, are the benefits of such research? It is my belief that it does have a valid place amongst the more traditional historical disciplines; that, as Tillhagen puts it: 'the result of folklife research might serve as a rejuvenation of our view of history.'[11]

Dorson has defined the scope of folklore as being to 'reconstruct a spiritual history of man, not as exemplified by the outstanding

11 C. Tillhagen, 'Reality and folklore research' in Bo Almqvist and ors. (ed.), *Hereditas* (Dublin, 1975), p. 329.

works of poets and thinkers but as represented by the more or less inarticulate voices of the "folk" [12], and elsewhere wrote that 'Students relish folklore because it informs them of the human values and outlooks of common people so often missing from standard subjects in the humanities and social sciences.' [13] It is my belief that students of law are increasingly being lulled into considering law and the legal system in a vacuum. Most aspects of law are taught with the underlying assumption that how it works in principle is necessarily how it works in practice: often, this is simply not the case. Subjects such as legal history, jurisprudence and criminology, which examine law in relation to its effects in the real world, are marginalised – the interests of a mere few. It is easy to get engrossed in studying particular areas of law; it is not so easy, nor so common, to attempt to think about law holistically – what is it, how is it perceived, what has it done, where is it going? Yet these are important questions. The common law system has been by no means universally successful or universally liked in Ireland, and neither has it been the sole means by which disputes have been settled over the last two and a half centuries. Customary courts, arbitration and mediation, clerical intervention, the use of oaths and truth-telling ordeals: all these things and more have at one stage or another assumed the role which the common law arrogates to itself as the arbiter of justice, the instrument for resolving conflicts. Even where the common law has been the chosen system, that has not always meant the simple hearing of evidence and applying of legal rules or precedents. Bribery of officials, the use of 'influence' by powerful societal figures, even resort to occult or superstitious practices: these have all reared their heads at one time or another, and where 'official' historical sources fail us we must turn to the voices of popular tradition if we are to learn anything at all about such matters.

The twentieth century has seen a recognition, through the works of Pound and others, of the important contribution which sociology can make to jurisprudential thought. Cotterrell, in the introduction to his work, *The sociology of law*, says that 'law is too

---

12 Dorson, in A. Krappe, *The science of folklore* (London, 1962), p. xv.
13 Dorson, *Folklore and fakelore*, p. 3.

important a social phenomenon to be analysed in a way that isolates it from other aspects of society and makes impossible an understanding of its social character, the complexity of its relations with other social phenomena, its "reality" as a part of life and not merely as a technique of professional practice.'[14] The legal philosopher Ronald Dworkin has also sought to highlight the need for analysis of how law and the legal system impinge on the lives of individuals in a general sense.[15]

However, sociology is a relatively young discipline, and detailed research is scant. In those times and places where dedicated academic research has not been carried out, I believe folklore and folk literature to be the best tools available for such analysis. There is much truth to be found in folk narratives, though it may not appear on the surface. Once the limitations and characteristics of the medium are known, it is possible to gain insights of value into the minds and hearts of ordinary people in Ireland over the last two and a half centuries. Even where accounts are not truthful, the recurrence of certain archetypes can tell us something of the attitudes of a people who were entertained by such stories: for instance, the story of two lawyers conspiring to 'fleece' their respective clients. The archetype runs as follows: two neighbours engage in a dispute, which escalates until both are willing to go to law. Some time before the case is due to come on for hearing, one of the parties is asked by his lawyer to carry a note to the lawyer acting for the opposing party. Becoming suspicious, he decides to read the note, and discovers that the two lawyers have been conspiring, not to settle the dispute but to prolong it in order to inflate their fees – thereby 'fleecing' the two disputants. Upon discovery of this plot, the parties get together and resolve the dispute themselves, informally. The likelihood of this story being true is remote; but the mere fact of its existence, coupled with the fact that it recurs in several different parts of the country at different times, points to a widespread attitude of distrust and suspicion towards lawyers and their activities.[16]

14 R. Cotterrell, *Sociology of law: an introduction* (2nd ed., London, 1992), pp. 1–2.
15 Ronald Dworkin, *Law's empire* (Cambridge, Mass., 1986).
16 See below, pp. 72–73, and appendix 3.

TRAVEL LITERATURE

Travel books and diaries have also proved a useful source of information, on two levels. Firstly, they can contain much information about folk customs and beliefs pertinent to law and the legal system. Secondly, they can provide a useful factual contrast or support for claims made by folk interviewees. A particularly rich source in this regard is the travel writing of Henry Inglis, who journeyed the length and breadth of Ireland during the spring, summer and autumn of 1834. Born in 1795, the son of a Scottish lawyer, Henry David Inglis spent the early part of his career in business, before discovering his true talent at the age of thirty, with the publication of his first travelogue, *Tales of the Ardennes*, under the pseudonym Derwent Conway. It was a runaway success; after which he became a full-time writer until his death in 1835 – the year in which his *Journey throughout Ireland* was first published. Along with lavish descriptions of scenery, a travel writer such as Inglis was expected to give insights into the 'soul' of the country: the traits of its people, the stuff of their everyday lives, their beliefs, customs and opinions. Perhaps because of his family upbringing, Inglis felt that by far the best way to judge the moral temperature of a nation was to visit local courthouses, and he included a number of these in his itinerary: 'Everywhere in Ireland, when the opportunity presented itself, I attended the sessions.... Upon no occasion, is so much insight at so small an expenditure of time and labour [gained] into the character of the peasantry; and even into the state of the country.'[17]

Inglis's diligence bore fruit in the form of a number of surprising observations concerning the behaviour of the Irish peasantry in and out of court – observations that will be examined in the course of this book. In reading his work and that of other foreign visitors, however, it must be borne in mind that they were not without their own prejudices. To a greater or lesser degree, every commentator brings the prism of their own culture and values to bear on their subject (I no less than others). As with the *seanchaí* by an Irish fireside, the primary goal of these writers was not

17 Henry Inglis, *Ireland in 1834* (London, 1835), pp. 145, 253.

truth, but entertainment. We must be alert for signs of exaggeration, selectivity or even pure fiction in their accounts. Once this awareness is maintained, then travel writings can constitute a useful source of supplementary material.

FICTION

Finally, I turn to works of fiction, and what may be learned from them. There is, primarily in the United States but also in Britain and Ireland, a growing scholastic movement which is turning to 'law in literature' for jurisprudential material. As Geary and Morison put it, 'The idea is that literary texts, whether dealing directly with the legal system or more obliquely with themes that are shared with law, contain insights about the legal order that are not available in the sort of material to which the legal theorist is normally limited.'[18] In this context, I shall refer principally to the works of certain nineteenth-century authors such as Gerald Griffin, William Carleton or the Banim brothers, who set their novels and short stories in rural Ireland, and whose talent for observation makes their work of special interest to the social historian. Obviously, we are not concerned with artistic merit; several of the more 'useful' writers have but a middling critical reputation (although William Carleton has been undergoing something of a renaissance in recent years). Neither do we expect to find unswerving devotion to the objective pursuit of truth, or to the understanding of a nation in all its complexity. But those who have the patience to trawl through pages of sometimes indifferent prose will find hidden gems of description or comment which can refract the light of popular culture in a way hitherto unseen, and which may in the process confirm or give the lie to conclusions suggested by folk sources.

Several writers exhibit a flair for accurate description and an enthusiasm to capture the life they saw around them in literary form, among them Anthony Trollope, whose 'Irish' novels form

18 Ray Geary and John Morison, 'An illustration of the literary approach to the study of law: the "mysteries" novels of the nineteenth century and the "Troubles thriller"', in N. Dawson, D. Greer and P. Ingram (ed.), *One hundred and fifty years of Irish law* (Belfast, 1996), p. 105.

the subject of a legal paper by W. N. Osborough. Osborough cites Trollope's major achievement in this context as being '... his preservation in a literary format of so much of the passing scene, things taken for granted at the time, surviving accounts of which are rare but which, for no especial reason, attracted the attention of a gifted author with an observant eye.'[19] It is this quality we seek in the writers whose work we shall examine.

Gerald Griffin (1803–40), a short story writer and novelist chiefly known for his tale of romance and murder, *The collegians* (1828), has a similar eye for detail. Griffin, though Irish, was not of peasant stock; he came from an urban, middle-class background. But what he lacks in experience of the culture of rural Ireland, he makes up for with keen observation. Lacking a certain empathy with peasant attitudes, he is nonetheless faithful in reproducing them. Take for instance the central characters in his greatest novel, *The collegians*. Griffin was a man of strong moral and religious convictions, and in the following excerpt from a letter to his brother, he left no doubt as to who he felt was the real hero of the book. But his knowledge of his readership left him equally convinced as to which character would in fact prove most popular:

One would wish to draw a good moral from the tale and yet it seems impossible to keep people's feelings in the way they ought to go in. Look at these two characters of Kyrle Daly and Hardress Cregan for example. Kyrle Daly, full of high principle, prudent, amiable and affectionate; not wanting in spirit, nor free from passion; but keeping his passions under control; thoughtful, kindhearted and charitable; a character in every way deserving of our esteem. Hardress Cregan, his mother's proud pet, nursed in the very lap of passion, and ruined by indulgence – not without good feelings, but forever abusing them, having a full sense of justice and honour, but shrinking like a craven from their dictates; following pleasure headlong, and eventually led into crimes of the blackest dye, by total absence of self-control. Take Kyrle Daly's character in what way you will, it is infinitely preferable; yet I will venture to say, nine out of ten

---

19 Osborough, 'The lawyers of the Irish novels of Anthony Trollope', in W.N. Osborough and Daire Hogan (ed.), *Brehons, serjeants and attorneys* (Dublin, 1990), p. 249.

who read this book will prefer Hardress Cregan; just because he is a fellow of high mettle, with a dash of talent about him.[20]

While he may not have agreed with the taste of the majority in this regard, Griffin was astute enough to be aware of it. Even within the pages of the novel itself, he writes that

Kyrle Daly, though highly popular among his inferiors and dependants, had only a second place in their affection, compared with his friend Hardress. A generosity utterly reckless and unreasoning is a quality that in all seasons has wrought most powerfully upon the inclinations of the Irish peasantry, who are themselves more distinguished for quick and kindly feeling than for a just perception of moral excellence. Because, therefore, the flow of generosity in Hardress Cregan was never checked nor governed by motives of prudence nor of justice, while good sense and reason regulated that of Kyrle Daly, the estimation in which they were held was proportionately unequal. The latter was spoken of as 'a good master'; but Hardress was their darling.[21]

It is this ability to observe from outside the characteristics and foibles of the Irish peasantry that makes Griffin's work a rewarding source for folk historians. A further bonus exists for those students of law and order in the late eighteenth and early nineteenth centuries, for Griffin was greatly concerned with the violence and contempt for law which he saw as rife within Irish society. Violence is a recurring theme in his two collections of short stories, *Holland-tide* and *Tales of the Munster festivals*, and *The collegians* itself is based around a notorious real-life murder in County Limerick, the so-called '*Cailín Bán*' ('*Colleen Bawn*') murder.[22] Griffin also takes it upon himself to reveal the mixture of justice, bribery, influence and superstition which pervaded the operation of the legal system in rural areas; to describe the acclaim accorded to people (such as Poll and Phil Naughten in *The collegians*) who could make the law an ass; and to show how he

20 Gerald Griffin, *The collegians* (New York, 1979), pp. xv–xvi. *The collegians* was first published in 1829.
21 ibid., p. 59.
22 See below, pp. 47–48.

believed the system was biased in favour of the rich and powerful. We shall have cause to return to all these topics during the course of this study.

Now comes a special case; a unique talent of whom it may be said without exaggeration that he poured the heart and soul of rural Ireland into his pages: I speak of William Carleton. The difference between Carleton and Griffin could not be more stark: what Griffin observed, Carleton *lived*. Griffin strove to step outside his own bourgeois culture and understand the peasant; Carleton intuitively understood and empathised with the Irish peasant, and try as he might to 'better himself' in different ways and to renounce 'uncivilised' values, he remained a peasant at heart, albeit one blessed with a considerable gift for writing, and significant critical faculties. Yeats wrote: 'The history of a nation is not in parliaments and battlefields, but in what the people say to each other on fair days and high days, and in how they farm, and quarrel, and go on pilgrimage. These things Carleton recorded.'[23]

William Carleton (1794–1869) was born and raised in a peasant family from Co. Tyrone, in the north of Ireland. According to his own autobiographical account, he was blessed with a father especially rich in his knowledge of the beliefs, superstitions and tales of rural Irish society:

And so strongly were all these impressed upon my mind, by frequent repetition on his part, and the indescribable delight they gave me on mine, that I have hardly ever since heard, during a tolerably enlarged intercourse with Irish society, both educated and uneducated – with the antiquary, the scholar, or the humble senachie – any single tradition, usage, or legend, that, as far as I can at present recollect, was perfectly new to me or unheard before, in some similar or cognate dress.[24]

23 W.B. Yeats, *Representative Irish tales* (London, 1979), p. 363. *Representative Irish tales* was first published in 1891.
24 William Carleton, *Traits and stories of the Irish peasantry* (New York, 1979), 1st series, ii, p. ix. The first series of *Traits and stories* (consisting of two volumes) appeared anonymously in 1830. Its unexpected success led to the publication of a second, three-volume series in 1832, this time crediting Carleton as the author. In 1844, both series were combined in a two-volume 'new edition', which also boasted a new introduction by Carleton himself, new illustrations and added footnotes. The version I shall generally be referring to is a 1979 reproduction of the original two series.

So when at length he came to try his hand at writing, Carleton, with his background and experiences, was uniquely placed to record the condition and character of the Irish peasantry with a loving accuracy never matched before or since. As Sloan points out, 'the accuracy, truth and realism of Carleton's best works have always been something of a cliché among his readers and admirers.'[25]

His work is by no means flawless: having converted to Protestantism, Carleton was wont to suppress his true talents in an effort to proselytise by ridiculing the religious and pagan practices he had grown up with. More often than not, however – and especially in the volumes of *Traits and stories of the Irish peasantry* – the artist triumphs over the preacher, and here we find wonderful, natural portraits of rural Irish society; of the hopes, dreams, fears and foibles of the people he grew up with, whose influence he could never quite escape. For all his education, literary success and religious conversion, Carleton remained what he began life as: a Tyrone peasant, steeped in religion, custom, superstition, violence, celebration, and the peculiar logic of the common people. Unlike more anglicised authors such as Maria Edgeworth or Mrs S.C. Hall, who wrote predominantly with their English audience in mind, Carleton identified much more with his characters than with his readership – the difference between sympathy and empathy. While not the only author to come from peasant stock, his passionate, unquenchable love for his people, together with his talent for observation and detailed description, place him head and shoulders above the Banim brothers and other similar writers. Much use will be made of his work in later chapters of this book.

IRISH COURTS SYSTEM

Finally, I feel it necessary to include a brief overview of the courts system as it existed in Ireland over the relevant period – focusing on courts of local jurisdiction, around which most stories and opinions are based. The most important figures were the justices

25 B. Sloan, *The pioneers of Anglo-Irish fiction, 1800–1850* (New York, 1986), p. 145.

of the peace – unpaid amateurs, who sat at quarter sessions, at petty sessions or on their own. Sitting in quarter sessions gave them a considerably wider jurisdiction than that enjoyed by a single justice. In England, the typical justice of the peace was a local landowner, a gentleman of some substance. But in Ireland the phenomenon of absenteeism amongst the landed gentry led in some cases to a bench of a rather different composition. McDowell wrote that 'At the beginning of the nineteenth century it was said that in some parts of the country highly unsuitable persons were placed on the bench. For instance it was said that in one disturbed area (in county Cork) the justices were "brewsters, maltsters, distillers and rackrent landlords."'[26] Thomas Reid wrote of the Sligo magistracy in 1822 that the title, 'justice of the peace' was quite misplaced; 'Disturber of the Peace would be much nearer the truth'.[27]

A general process of reform was instituted in 1822; this included the formalising of the magistrates' individual jurisdictions through the development of the practice of holding petty sessions – in which the single magistrate became two or more, acting together. The Petty Sessions Act 1827[28] regularised this still further, requiring justices to sit at fixed times, with a clerk, and to keep records. However, it is worth bearing in mind that the majority of justices of the peace remained Protestant: according to McDowell, even by 1886, a mere 1,200 out of 5,000 magistrates were Catholic.[29]

For much of the eighteenth century, allegations of incompetence and susceptibility to bribery were directed at many justices of the peace, not only by the indigenous population, but also by foreign observers. The solution, as many saw it, was the introduction of paid professionals. By an act of 1787, the Lord Lieutenant could, in certain disturbed areas, appoint a barrister to be 'a constant assistant' to the justices at quarter sessions. He would be paid for his activities. This experiment was deemed a success, and subsequently extended to cover the entire country. The assistant barrister

---

26 R.B. McDowell, 'The Irish courts of law, 1801–1914', in *IHS*, x (1957), 371; and see too W.N. Osborough, 'The Irish legal system, 1796–1877', in Caroline Costello (ed.), *The Four Courts: 200 years* (Dublin, 1996), p. 33.
27 Thomas Reid, *Travels in Ireland in the year 1822* (London, 1823), p. 369.
28 7 & 8 Geo. IV, c.67.
29 Loc. cit. (n. 26), p. 372.

could also hear civil claims involving less than £20[30] – a jurisdiction which was steadily enlarged as time went by.

In 1822, after a number of limited experiments, a breed of stipendiary magistrates began to emerge. Their exact functions remained unclear: an 1846 government memorandum simply said that they were to make themselves as useful as possible – in particular by attending petty sessions and local fairs.[31] These individuals became known as resident magistrates, and by 1860 numbered 72.

By the middle of the nineteenth century, there existed a confusing variety of courts exercising a local jurisdiction. McDowell provides a useful summary, which I feel is worth reproducing in full, despite its length:

Dublin had four local courts – the court of quarter sessions, the lord mayor's court, the mayor and sheriff's court, and the court of conscience. The court of quarter sessions had cognizance of all crimes (except treason) committed within the city's boundaries; the lord mayor's court exercised a summary jurisdiction in a number of minor offences and settled small disputes (such as those between servants and masters over wages or between masters and apprentices); the mayor and sheriff's court had cognizance of all personal actions, and the court of conscience settled disputes which involved less than forty shillings. The judges in the court of quarter sessions were the lord mayor, the recorder and the senior aldermen, in the mayor and sheriff's court the lord mayor, the sheriff and the recorder, in the lord mayor's court the lord mayor himself, and in the court of conscience the lord mayor of the preceding year. But theory and practice did not altogether coincide. Most serious offences, instead of being tried at quarter sessions, were reserved for the commission court (held before two judges of a superior court). At quarter sessions the recorder sat alone, and in the mayor and sheriff's court he heard motions sitting alone. The business of this latter court had greatly decreased during the early nineteenth century, as cases could be removed to a superior court. The court of conscience was remarkable for the ease with which a rehearing could be secured by the defeated party, with a consequent increase of fees for the officers of the court.

Cork, Limerick, Londonderry, Kilkenny and Waterford all had a quarter sessions court dealing with criminal cases, a mayor and sheriff's

---

30 27 Geo. III, c.40; 36 Geo. III, c.25.
31 McDowell, p. 373.

court (a court of record) dealing with civil disputes and a court of conscience. In Carrickfergus and Galway there was a quarter sessions court and a Tholsel court which dealt with civil disputes. Waterford had these courts and a mayor's court; and two boroughs, Kinsale and Youghal, which were not counties of boroughs, nevertheless had quarter sessions courts and record courts with wide jurisdiction. In about twenty-three boroughs there were courts of limited jurisdiction presided over by the head of the corporation. The little business they had was usually concerned with the quick collection of small debts. At least thirty other boroughs seem to have at some time possessed similar courts, but during the eighteenth and early nineteenth centuries they ceased to function.

Finally there were the manor courts which possessed a threefold jurisdiction, a common law jurisdiction ranging in amount from five marks to £200, exercised according to the forms of the superior courts; the jurisdiction of a court baron which could be exercised comparatively expeditiously; and finally a statutory jurisdiction granted during the eighteenth and early nineteenth centuries of a simple, speedy kind for the collection of small debts.[32]

In 1837, there were approximately 200 manor courts spread throughout the country. Their popularity during the eighteenth and early nineteenth centuries owed much to their informal atmosphere (some were held in public houses, the publicans recognising that a court day could be good for business), their willingness to conduct proceedings in Irish, and the fact that they were relatively inexpensive to avail of. The occasional disorder and abandonment of legal formality may simply have added to the amusement and enthusiasm of the rural Irish litigant.[33] In the end, however, the unregulated nature of the proceedings, together with the ignorance and caprice which many seneschals (the name given to judges of these courts) displayed, led to a decline in usage. The growth in number and efficiency of the assistant barristers' courts and petty sessions ensured that, by the 1840s, the manor courts were in permanent decline. They were suppressed altogether by an 1859 act of parliament.[34]

32 ibid., pp. 375–76.
33 ibid., pp. 375–77.
34 22 Vict., c.14.

From the foregoing summary of the Irish courts system, one can draw attention to certain factors which, in themselves, are likely to have influenced popular views on the machinery of justice. The profusion of local courts, each possessed of their own particular jurisdiction; the existence of unpredictable disparities between their ostensible structure and the manner in which they in fact operated; the broad variations to be found in legal knowledge and in formality of procedure (both from court to court and from place to place); all these things tend to give an impression of muddle and confusion which can hardly have fostered a sense of the majesty of the law. The more courts there were, the greater the opportunities for lawyers to spend their time arguing over points of procedure, and for cases to be decided on such technicalities, without reference to what ordinary people would consider 'the real issues'. As well as distancing the law from the 'common sense' opinion of the man or woman in the street, this made it difficult for the average person to predict with certainty the outcome of any litigation.

Taking all these things into consideration, one might expect to find in the folklore archives a general wariness of courts and lawyers, coupled, perhaps, with a certain cynicism concerning the relationship between the law and justice. Whether this is in fact the case, shall be examined in the next chapter.

CHAPTER TWO

Law, justice and the Irish

CENTRAL TO THIS study is the theme of the extent to which law impinged on the lives and thoughts of rural Irish men and women. What did people think of when they thought of 'law'? How often did they go to court? What were their reasons for doing so? What was the popular attitude towards obsessive or crank plaintiffs? What tactics did people employ, in and out of court, to promote their own interests and agendas? What did they think of lawyers? Did the ordinary rural inhabitant enjoy being in court, or was it a fearful experience, to be avoided at all costs? As might be expected, there are no simple answers to these questions. Contradictory views abound, both within and outside of folk culture.

Literary fiction provides us with two broad stereotypes. On the one hand, we have the image of the downtrodden peasant, oppressed by laws of which he or she is ignorant. This picture has for a long time dominated Irish historical writing – as, for instance, in the novel *Trinity* (1976) by the American writer Leon Uris. As the events of the novel unfold, Uris's Catholic, nineteenth-century narrator depicts a people entirely crushed beneath the heel of a foreign legal system, a system in which their lack of understanding crippled any hope of victory:

All those connected to law – the Crown and the courts and the soldiers reading edicts – were bullies forcing us into a game played by their rules spoken in a language only they understood. We knew little about our rights and nothing at all about the ability to use law. Law remained a bludgeon owned by Lord Hubble and the Protestants, and we'd no manner of defence against their judges all dressed up like princes and the documents all covered with seals.[1]

---

1   Leon Uris, *Trinity* (London, 1976), pp. 30–31.

Uris sees the rural Irish as suffering from two great disabilities: an ignorance of the common law courts system, and a lack of fluency in English – especially lawyers' English. Reading between the lines, one also senses a certain fear – a recognition that the law was a powerful English weapon, which could destroy a poor man's life as easily as a gun. This is the black-and-white view which pervades Irish nationalist history and literature, and seems to have been common countrywide. Desmond Keenan, in his study of the Catholic church in nineteenth-century Ireland, cites a passage from an 1825 parliamentary enquiry as evidence of a general sense amongst the rural Irish that they were a persecuted people. It was said that 'there is little doubt that there was a feeling of oppression ... the sense of grievance of the peasantry was marked and more strongly felt by the lower orders, even if they were vague about the actual details of the oppression.'[2]

But if we turn to the much earlier stories of Somerville and Ross (1928) a very different picture presents itself. Somerville and Ross wrote a series of short stories based around the life and activities of one Major Yeates, a (fictional) English gentleman appointed to Ireland to act as a resident magistrate (R.M.). What we read is a far cry from the gloom and oppression of *Trinity*: here it is Major Yeates who is at sea – alone in a strange culture, constantly fighting to stem a veritable flood of half-truth, manipulation, bribery and feuding between clans. An appearance of ignorance is maintained by the indigenous Irish, but the major quickly finds out that this is far from the truth; though they may not be better versed in law than he, many are extremely adept at bending the language and mechanisms of legal proceedings to their own advantage. In *Trinity*, ignorance of the English language is a crippling handicap; in the *Irish R.M.* stories, a feigned unfamiliarity with its subtleties can be a potent weapon for litigants and witnesses. In and out of the courtroom, Major Yeates is often found struggling to cope with a language which, though nominally English, possesses layers of meaning and counter-meaning completely alien to his experience. In the following passage from

2 Desmond Keenan, *The Catholic church in nineteenth-century Ireland* (Dublin, 1983), p. 27.

one of the earlier tales he pens a brief description of the difficulties of his working life:

Daily ... I set forth for the Petty Sessions Courts of my wide district; daily, in the inevitable atmosphere of wet frieze and perjury, I listened to indictments of old women who plucked geese alive, of publicans whose hospitality to their friends broke forth uncontrollably on Sunday afternoons, of 'parties' who, in the language of the police sergeant, were subtly defined as 'not to say dhrunk, but in good fighting thrim.'[3]

Obviously, this is comic writing, and as such is prone to exaggeration. Yet one may equally accuse Uris of exaggerating in his darker vision of Irish peasant life. The truth lies somewhere between these extremes.

Leaving the world of pure fiction, we turn to Jarlath Waldron's historical reconstruction of one of Ireland's most famous, real-life murder trials, that which concerned the Maamtrasna killings. We look first at Myles Joyce, a man tried, convicted and subsequently hanged for the murders, though many believed him to have been innocent. Waldron describes his court appearance as follows:

As Myles Joyce took his stand in Green Street Courthouse on that Friday afternoon, 17th November 1882, he was truly in a foreign land. Foreign-looking people, who surrounded him, speaking a foreign language, were talking about him and were determined to settle within a few hours whether he would be allowed to live any longer, or be allowed home to his own valley and to his wife and children. But he, Myles, may just as well have been in China, for not one solitary word of the English did he understand. Except for a moment or two at the beginning and end he did not have the benefit of an interpreter nor would he be brought into this hectic discussion about his life and his right to life.[4]

Myles fits the *Trinity* type of the poor, ignorant Irishman, unaware of what was happening before his eyes, and eventually to die for a crime most people believed he did not commit. By way of contrast, let us now look at Anthony Joyce, a key witness at the

---

3   E. Somerville and M. Ross, *Complete experiences of an Irish R.M.* (London, 1970), p. 10.
4   Jarlath Waldron, *Maamtrasna* (Dublin, 1992), p. 108.

trial (and one who is believed to have lied considerably during his testimony):

Anthony Joyce, the leader of the 'independent witnesses', took the stand ... He would not answer when asked did he speak English – a well-known ploy in courtrooms. Many non-English speakers could understand it adequately, but to think out their replies while the interpreter was translating, they feigned total ignorance.[5]

Anthony is more in the canny *Irish R.M.* mould, although the outcome of his trickery is far more tragic than anything Somerville and Ross would have written. He knows exactly where he is and what he is doing there, and uses every little ploy available to him to turn the outcome to his advantage.

So then, as we might have expected, we find the stereotypes of both Uris and Somerville and Ross are founded to some extent in reality – at least in Waldron's interpretation. But does one have more of the truth than the other? Which was more common: the scheming, litigious peasant of the *Irish R.M.*, or the timorous, ignorant wretch portrayed by Uris?

Turning to the travel literature of the nineteenth century, we find much to support the view that Irish people, by and large, had little fear of law; rather, they combined a passion for the cut and thrust of legal proceedings with an innate understanding of how to use the system for their own benefit and amusement. Some writers professed astonishment at the level of legal understanding and sophistication to which the Irish peasant not infrequently rose. Blake, the author of *Letters from the Irish highlands* (1825), wrote that,

Upon this subject, which is of such vital importance to them, they often show a knowledge, not only of the common points, but also of the technical niceties, which is far beyond anything that would be met with in an English peasant. They understand exactly how far they may go without hazarding the animadversion of a magistrate, and often as they

5   ibid., p. 64. See also *R. v. Burke* (1858) 8 Cox CC 44. For further discussion of language and interpreters in the courtroom, see chapter 5 below, at pp. 95–98.

exceed the bounds of moderation, yet still oftener do they verture upon the very verge, and there stop short, to the surprise and admiration of all spectators.[6]

Writing in 1806, the English barrister John Carr (1771–1832) described the enthusiasm for law which he saw in Killarney:

Every Irishman thinks himself somewhat of a lawyer, and is, from the little vanity of displaying his logical skill, more than from a spirit of litigation, uncommonly fond of being a party to a cause, or forming one of the auditory of a court of justice; hence in Ireland the quarter-sessions never fail to bring an uncommon number of people together.[7]

Thirty years later, Henry Inglis described scenes at a typical Irish assizes, which to us today are more redolent of some celebrity appearance than of the sober atmosphere of a court of law:

Dense crowds are collected at the door of every attorney's office, and no one of this brotherhood can walk a yard, without having his sleeve pulled by half-a-dozen 'boys' or women, all interested for or against somebody; and entreating his honour to get them justice.[8]

He observed generally 'a great spirit of litigation, and a good deal of quibbling'.[9] Thackeray, in his *Irish sketchbook*, described scenes at a petty sessions court in Roundstone, Co. Galway. What he observed moved him to comment that 'Mr O'Connell,[10] who is always crying out "Justice for Ireland", finds strong supporters among the Roundstonians, whose love of justice for themselves is inordinate'.[11]

The observations of the travel writers, however, stand in stark contrast to the predominant voices of popular tradition. In fact,

6 M. Blake, *Letters from the Irish highlands* (London, 1825), pp. 197–98.
7 John Carr, *The stranger in Ireland* (London, 1806), p. 359.
8 Inglis, *Ireland in 1834*, p. 281.
9 ibid., p. 145.
10 Daniel O'Connell (1775–1847), famous Irish lawyer and political leader. Spearheaded campaigns for Catholic emancipation (granted in 1829) and for repeal of the Act of Union. Popularly known as 'the Liberator' or 'the Counsellor'.
11 William Makepeace Thackeray, *Irish sketchbook, 1842* (Belfast, 1985), p. 218.

the majority of popular sayings advocate steering clear of the courts wherever possible: 'The least of the law is the best of it';[12] 'I ngan fhios don dlí ab fhearr a bheith ann';[13] 'The man that was fond of law would get his fill of it';[14] 'The first loss is the best';[15] ' "Keep out of the law" was a motto that was cherished by great numbers';[16] 'Ná sáruigh naoidhe le dlighe de fhriotal gan áird; Dar láimh mo choim tá nídh nár thuigis le fagháil';[17] 'It's better to keep the peace than go to law... any sort of peace is better than going to law'.[18] A Monaghan man told one folk collector that 'The average man and woman had a horror of law cases, and if they could get a way out of it they wouldn't go to law', adding that old men would be proud to tell you they never saw the inside of a courthouse.[19]

How can we reconcile these statements with the reality as perceived from outside? One might be tempted to assume that the sayings do not relate to the first half of the nineteenth century (from where most of our journalistic sources come), but to some other, less litigious age. It is possible (though perhaps unlikely) that this period was unique in terms of enthusiasm for legal action. We cannot say for sure. But there are other ways in which the proverbs set out above might be accounted for. These ways are worth setting out at this stage.

A DISLIKE OF LAW

Crank litigants

Some of the above warnings to steer clear of law follow stories of people who in the eyes of the rural populace displayed the niggling,

---

12 IFC Ms. Vol. 1195, p. 372.
13 'It's best to be without knowledge of law': IFC Ms. Vol. 238, p. 306.
14 IFC Ms. Vol. 1197, p. 93.
15 IFC Ms. Vol. 1197, p. 215.
16 IFC Ms. Vol. 1193, p. 321.
17 'Do not injure anyone in law for the sake of a dishonourable word; I pledge my heart that thou will obtain a thing thou knowest not of': Daniel Corkery quoting from (and translating) the poet Aogán Ó Rathaille, in *The hidden Ireland* (Dublin, 1925), p. 190.
18 IFC Ms. Vol. 1197, p. 21.
19 IFC Ms. Vol. 1096, p. 346.

petty-minded recourse to litigation which characterises the crank plaintiff. A number of such characters emerge from the folklore archives: Black Mick from Limerick, who by all accounts was so frequently before the courts that 'even court officials noted his absence from the usual session';[20] a man named Tormey from Cavan, who through a combination of experience and sheer bloody-minded persistence won case after case before finally bankrupting himself in a long drawn-out battle with his brother over land bequeathed to that brother by their father.[21] Another fine specimen was discovered by Thackeray at Roundstone:

Last on the list which I took down, came a man who will make the fortune of the London attorney, that I hope is on his way hither. A rather old curly headed man, with a sly smile perpetually lying on his face (the reader may give whatever interpretation he please to the 'lying') – he comes before the Court almost every fortnight they say, with a complaint of one kind or other. His present charge was against a man for breaking into his court-yard, and wishing to take possession of the same. It appeared however that he, the defendant and another lived in a row of houses – the plaintiff's house was, however, first built, and as his agreement specified that the plot of ground behind his house should be his likewise, he chose to imagine that the plot of ground behind all the three houses was his, and built his turf-stack against his neighbour's window. The magistrates of course pronounced against this ingenious discoverer of wrongs, and he left the court still smiling and twisting round his little wicked eyes, and declaring solemnly that he would put in an *appale*.[22]

Such characters could attain considerable notoriety amongst lawyers and laymen alike: for example, the *Irish Law Times* of 5 March 1899 noted in its 'Echoes of the Courts' column that

Miss McManus, a well-known lady litigant from County Monaghan, appeared in person and conducted her own case before Mr Justice Meredith on Wednesday last in the Land Commission Court. This lady is a familiar figure at every Monaghan Assizes for years past. In the present case she was not successful.[23]

---

20 IFC Ms. Vol. 1193, p. 323.
21 IFC Ms. Vol. 1197, pp. 1, 161.
22 Thackeray, *Irish sketchbook* pp. 221–22.
23 *ILT & SJ*, xxxii (1899), 110. In Maurice Healy's *The old Munster circuit*

One would not imagine such characters to be too popular; a man from the border area between Cavan and Meath told one folk collector that 'The man that was fond of law was looked down on by the rest of the people and got the name of being contrary and hard to put up with. You'd meet an odd one like that.'[24] Of course, we do not know whether over-eager plaintiffs were looked down on because of their constant recourse to law, or whether their willingness to use the courts was in response to an already existing unpopularity. Were they disliked because they sued, or did they sue because they were disliked? And even if their litigiousness was the cause of their unpopularity, all that tells us is that they were damned for using the courts more often than the average: it sheds no light on what that average was. As we have seen, the indications from foreign sources are that it was considerably higher than in most other European countries throughout the eighteenth and nineteenth centuries.

Ignorance

A lack of knowledge of legal rules and procedures is a sensible ground for avoiding lawsuits, and it may be that such ignorance engendered the fear of law which is evident in the folk proverbs. But the massed evidence of Inglis, Thackeray, Carr and others, that Irish people were exceptionally well-versed in law, is compelling; and I feel that some of the other factors considered can better explain the folk proverbs we are considering.

Bias / prejudice

Whatever the reality of the situation, the use of bribery and 'influence' was believed to have been rampant throughout the Irish court system. Many folk stories and sayings take it as given that judges were biased in favour of an elite – be they landlords, policemen, Protestants or freemasons. Hence, the only way for a

---

(Cork, 1979), p. 46 (first published 1939), there is a reference to a lady named Miss Anthony, who, in the time of his father, 'plagued' the courts on a regular basis, without the assistance of solicitor or counsel. She is also referred to in A.M. Sullivan's memoirs, *The last serjeant* (London, 1952), pp. 33–34.
24 IFC Ms. Vol. 1195, p. 369.

poor man to secure justice (or, more importantly, victory) was to reverse that bias, through bribery or the intercession of some powerful patron on their behalf.

Both folklore and other sources have much to say on the matter – so much so, that the topic merits treatment in a separate chapter.[25] For the present, it is sufficient to note that the advice to avoid litigation could have been addressed primarily to those who could not afford to compete on equal terms with the rich, the powerful, or the influential. Here we are not positing a fear of legal proceedings; rather, the proverbs are rooted in the experience and wisdom of a gambler who knows when to go the distance, and when to fold his cards. By this interpretation, 'do not go to court' becomes: 'do not go to court *unless you know you will win*'.

Expense / delay

The cost of legal proceedings, and in particular of lawyers' fees, is often decried in the folklore archives, and tales of greedy plaintiffs and protracted lawsuits usually end with one or both protagonists in penury – as in the case of Watty Tormey, referred to earlier.[26] A Cavan man, echoing the remarks of a number of others, said, 'I knew of people that had a big stock of cattle, maybe five or six cows and five or six herd of young cattle, and before they were done with the law suit they hadn't a four-footed beast in the field.'[27]

In a tale from Co. Clare, a man was warned (possibly by a fairy) to remain unknown to law; he disregarded this advice, and got involved in a dispute with a neighbour over damage to a boundary. The dispute went from court to court before eventually being settled at a loss to the man of £62: only then did he remember the warning.[28] From Limerick comes the story of two families who engaged in a lengthy court battle for ownership of an island in the middle of the river which separated their lands. The case dragged on into winter, and floods swept the island away. According to one account, 'Judge Adams strongly criticised

25 See below, chapter 3.
26 See above, p. 26.
27 IFC Ms. Vol. 1195, pp. 395–96.
28 IFC Ms. Vol. 861, p. 746. The storyteller reckons this to have taken place two generations previously.

the madness of expending a fortune on law proceedings over a holding that when it was in being couldn't support a snipe and had by now disappeared.'[29] Another account omits mention of Judge Adams, but says that the action was pursued as far as the 'Dublin courts', and the total legal costs borne by the parties were in excess of £100.[30] The same informant talks of law as 'something to be feared and mistrusted', and quotes a Fr Ryan as being fond of saying that 'whoever won a case the attorney always won it'.

Associated with expense is another factor: delay. Compared with the open-ended and essentially arbitral nature of customary procedures, the common law was supposed to provide definite and final answers to problems. But in the folk mind, it is often the common law actions which fail to produce a final settlement; many stories refer to disputes travelling between one court and another without resolution, with costs mounting up all the while. The longer a case drags on, the more obsessed the parties become with winning, and the less chance there is of ever restoring some kind of normal neighbourly relationship. Witness the outcome of a lengthy suit between Gleeson and Sweeney (two men from Cork): 'Bhí [Sweeney] briste ach má bhí ní raibh sé sásta gur bhris sé an fear eile chomh maith.'[31]

A rather improbable tale, told in Mayo and Galway, concerns two men who shared ownership of a sheep. One man sheared half the sheep, in order to get wool with which to make himself a pair of socks. That night a big storm broke, and the sheep sought shelter in a bramble bush: as luck would have it, it became ensnared, and died (whether from exposure or hunger is not clear). The second man sued the sock-maker, claiming that if he had not sheared half the sheep, the animal would not have felt cold, and would not as a consequence have felt the need to seek shelter in the brambles. The sock-maker put in a counterclaim, suggesting that if his partner had allowed him to shear the whole sheep, it

29 IFC Ms. Vol. 1193, p. 326. For more stories concerning this Judge Adams, see below, pp. 65–70.
30 IFC Ms. Vol. 1194, p. 535.
31 '[Sweeney] was broke but if he was he wasn't happy until he broke the other fellow as well.' IFC Ms. Vol. 45, p. 300.

wouldn't have become entangled in them. According to one version, no court arrived at an appropriate settlement of the matter; while another version ends by saying that they went from court to court until they had spent the equivalent in costs of ten sheep.[32]

A particularly ironic example of what is referred to as 'being broke through law' comes from Co. Kerry. A rich landowner named Muragrán sued his brother-in-law over some property. The case went on for a considerable time, until at length the barrister acting for him became a judge. The case came before him, and he held against his former client, saying, 'Now [I'm a judge] I'm sworn to do right.' Muragrán was left penniless and, no doubt, somewhat aggrieved at this turn of fate.[33] Another Kerry tale speaks of two families bankrupting themselves in litigation over farmland.[34] Two Cavan farmers recalled hearing of people who 'broke themselves at law' over a right of way: one said that the path in question was not wide enough to walk a horse through.[35] Another Cavan man told a story of two men named Flanagan and Larkin who ruined themselves in litigation over a broken gatepost.[36] From Monaghan comes the story of Carraher and Mahon, who rejected an offer by the storyteller to arbitrate, and subsequently bankrupted themselves in the courts.[37] One story from the south of Ireland (dated by the speaker at around 1860) has a supernatural twist to it: a tenant farmer was harvesting hay with his men when the 'fairy wind' came and stole the entire harvest. The farmer and the landowner were three years at law over it.[38]

Lawyers

Another reason for not going to court could be a dislike or distrust of lawyers. Lawyers have never been the most popular members of society; like undertakers, their business lies in other

32 IFC Ms. Vol. 238, p. 306; Vol. 489, p. 200.
33 IFC Ms. Vol. 702, p. 154.
34 IFC Ms. Vol. 1196, p. 496.
35 IFC Ms. Vol. 1197, pp. 92, 252.
36 IFC Ms. Vol. 1196, p. 177.
37 IFC Ms. Vol. 1096, p. 330.
38 IFC Ms. Vol. 45, p. 27.

people's misery. Neither are they helped by the abstruse nature of law itself, and the gulf which can sometimes separate popular and legal conceptions of 'justice'. Add to this the already mentioned factor of expense, plus the recurring suspicion that all lawyers are conspiring in secret to prolong the agony of their clients while they fatten their wallets – as evinced by the 'plucking the geese' tale, mentioned elsewhere[39] – and you have a strong argument (at least in the popular mind) for shunning their society at all costs. As with bribery and prejudice, both the countryman's view of lawyers, and the extent to which law and 'common sense' diverge in his mind, are topics which merit discussion in depth, and as a consequence will be dealt with in detail elsewhere.[40]

A LIKING FOR LAW

Having considered some of the factors which might have discouraged the Irish peasant from litigation, we should now consider possible explanations for the kind of enthusiasm for law which Inglis and others observed. To the academic lawyer, the answer to the question 'why do people go to court?' is obvious: people go there to seek justice in the application of the law. But to the social historian, the folklorist, the psychologist, or those involved daily in the grit and grime of the living court system, a number of other possibilities present themselves. Some of these are named by Simon Roberts in the course of his contribution to *Disputes and settlements*, a collection of essays edited by John Bossy:

People go to court-like agencies for a wide variety of purposes: for reasons of honour, to publicize some established position which requires no court ruling, or just to make things difficult for an enemy. The very notion of 'dispute' may not be apposite if the court is just being used as a platform from which to tell people something. In cases of this sort, the objective may not lie in terms of judgment at all.[41]

---

39 See above, p. 9, and below, pp. 72–73, and appendix 3.
40 See below, chapters 4, 8. In an historical context, see Wilfrid R. Prest, *The rise of the barristers: a social history of the English bar, 1590–1640* (Oxford, 1991), pp. 283–326.
41 Roberts, 'The study of dispute: anthropological perspectives', in John Bossy (ed.), *Disputes and settlements* (Cambridge, 1983), p. 23.

Communication

Pádraig Mac Gréine, in an article in *Béaloideas* on disputes and feuding within an itinerant or 'tinker' community, described their attitude to law as follows:

> It is not often they invoke the aid of the law.... That would be somewhat like invoking the aid of an enemy, which would be bad taste. Still, the tinker will often try to get his enemy into the clutch of the law while he himself remains in the background. When a tinker falls foul of the law, his relatives prove their loyalty by employing a solicitor in his defence. What is more, they pay the solicitor without a grumble.[42]

Several things emerge from this passage. Firstly, note the absence of any reference to justice or the final settlement of disputes. The 'tinker' community clearly see the legal system as inimical to their interests – an enemy to be avoided, rather than an impartial dispenser of justice. Problems are to be resolved within the community wherever possible, even if this leads to full-scale feuding between clans. Secondly, there are times when the law may be used, not to resolve disputes, but rather as one of a variety of weapons employed to defeat or humiliate one's adversary. Thirdly, in situations where a tinker falls into the clutches of the law, engaging a solicitor is an opportunity to demonstrate both the honour of the clan in staying loyal to its own, and the wealth of the clan in showing that they have sufficient financial resources to contest the case through 'official' channels.

A similar approach to law was noted by Chris Curtin, in a study of a small, isolated rural community in Co. Mayo, conducted in the mid-1970s. A dispute arose between two parties over a right of way. Following numerous arguments and violent incidents, both sides resorted to civil litigation. After four court appearances, the case was adjourned without resolution. Curtin points out that the dispute was one in a series of altercations between the families concerned, going back over many years:

> The legal mode of settlement was viewed as being expensive. It was held by those who knew the disputants as not providing a lasting solution,

42 'Some notes on tinkers and their cant' in *Béaloideas*, iv (1933–34), 260.

since the losing side would get no satisfaction and would probably seek revenge at a future date.... As locals assessed it, 'they were never on good terms anyway'. Put this way, the present dispute was a continuation, and an outcome of past conflicts. The dispute can also be viewed as a contest for each family's status in the village, and a public gesture to establish superior-inferior ranking in the village. In this way, the process of going to court was used by both families to prove that they had the resources to engage legal support.[43]

From these examples we can see the Irish courts fulfilling Roberts's predictions – being used not to settle conflict, but to increase it; not to seek justice, but rather as a platform from which to 'say' things to other people in one's community. This mentality is evident in Carleton's 'Battle of the factions' story, which narrates the tale of a dispute between the O'Callaghans and the O'Hallaghans over an 'island' twelve yards in diameter, created when the stream which separated the two families' lands changed course. Verbal arguments and abuse led gradually to more serious altercations:

They incarcerated our cattle, and we incarcerated theirs. They summoned us to their landlord, who was a magistrate; and we summoned them to ours, who was another.... Their landlord gave it in favour of them, and ours in favour of us. The one said he had law on his side; the other, that he had proscription [sic] and possession, length of time and usage. The two Squires then fought a challenge upon the head of it, and what was more singular, upon the disputed spot itself; the one standing on their side – the other on ours.

The two families then went to the law courts proper. Their journey through the courts lasted some eight or nine years, but hostilities did not cease during that time. Rather, they increased, and eventually the lawsuit was abandoned in favour of more brutal methods of dispute resolution:

Now during the lawsuit, we usually houghed and mutilated each other's cattle, according as they trespassed the premises. This brought on the

---

43 Curtin, 'Social order, interpersonal relations and disputes in a west of Ireland community', in Tomlinson & ors. (ed.), *Whose law and order? Aspects of crime and control in Irish society* (Belfast, 1988), p. 76, at p. 85.

usual concomitants of various battles, fought and won by both sides, and occasioned the lawsuit to be dropped, for we found it a mighty inconvenient matter to fight it out both ways.[44]

To the O'Callaghans and the O'Hallaghans, legal action was never likely to produce a final solution to the dispute, but was merely another device to annoy and frustrate one's enemies. It also provided an opportunity to display their financial resources and determination to win.[45]

It is possible that the restrictive nature of common law proceedings contributed to this pattern. As yet, little comparative research has been conducted into the sociological impact of common law tenets on colonised peoples. However, it is intriguing to note that in colonial India, the exclusion of certain types of evidence as being irrelevant or inadmissible seems to have prevented the court's judgment from being seen as final and comprehensive. Robert Kidder writes that

Restrictive rules of evidence violated the complex fabric of local relationships by allowing only proximate events to be mentioned in debate. The many strands of long-running disputes could be only partially captured within the narrow confines of a lawsuit. The result was that court decrees, rather than settling disputes, often added to the many already existing devices used by disputants to pursue their opponents.[46]

This use of the courts as a weapon against one's enemies seems equally well to describe the approach of the O'Callaghans and the O'Hallaghans, and of the travelling community as noted by Mac Gréine.

There is also a striking similarity with attitudes to law in sixteenth- and seventeenth-century England. Prest's description of that era in English legal life, and of the passion for litigation

44 Carleton, *Traits and stories*, 2nd series, i, p. 225.
45 In another of Carleton's tales from the same volume, a brawl takes place between the Dorans and the Flanagans at a wedding. While the fight broke out over a horse race, the real cause of the animosity was a recent lawsuit between them. ibid., p. 127.
46 Robert Kidder, 'Western law in India: external law and local response', in H. Johnson (ed.), *Social system and legal process* (San Francisco, 1978).

which seemed to engulf the whole country, resonates strongly with the descriptions of eighteenth- and nineteenth-century Ireland by Inglis and others. He writes:

Private law and litigation now play such a relatively insignificant part in the life of most modern western societies that a major effort of the imagination is required to grasp their central prominence in early modern times. The late sixteenth and early seventeenth centuries constituted possibly the most litigious era in English history, as well as a time when legal forms and institutions impinged upon almost every aspect of daily life. The explosion of litigation which so alarmed contemporaries was facilitated by the low initial cost of going to law, and the fact that attorneys commonly allowed their clients to sue on credit. If litigation was a favourite indoor sport of the period, as some historians have suggested, the players were not drawn solely from the landed élite, but also included peasants, artisans, craftsmen, and merchants.[47]

Furthermore, like the O'Callaghans, the O'Hallaghans and their ilk, the participants in this sport often did not have their minds on justice, but on injuring their opponents:

... legal process was easily exploited to prosecute malicious suits and pursue private vendettas.... As in sixteenth-century Castile, where litigation 'closely resembled feuding, except that ... contestants armed themselves not with arquebuses and rapiers but with a brace of lawyers and a torrent of legal briefs', going to law in early modern England was often rather a means of continuing and expanding conflicts rather than bringing them to an end.[48]

It has long been accepted that the courts serve a purpose of communicating messages from the State to its citizens: 'crime does not pay', 'contracts should be honoured', 'you owe a duty of care to your neighbour in certain situations', and the like. What is more surprising is that the courts should have been used by the citizens themselves to send messages to one another which the State had not sanctioned, and may well have been unaware of. We have seen how the courts could be used as an arena within which

47 Prest, *The rise of the barristers*, pp. 296–97.
48 ibid., pp. 299–300.

families and clans might boast of their power and resources. But perhaps the most shocking instance of using legal proceedings as a vehicle for private communication was the widely documented practice of women making false accusations of rape or sexual assault against a man, in order to encourage the accused to propose marriage to them. In one of the stories told of Daniel O'Connell, the great lawyer succeeds in defending a boy whom a girl has sought to 'trap' – presumably by some allegation of sexual misconduct.[49] Touring Ireland in 1813, the Revd James Hall found two unfortunate young men languishing in Longford gaol on charges of rape:

Among others, in the jail of Longford, I found two young men, accused of committing rapes. Virtuous as the young women of Ireland in general are, it has become, it seems, too common for a young woman to swear a rape against a young man, when, having been too familiar, he is not disposed to marry her. This is also sometimes done to extort money; and some young men, though innocent, rather choose to marry than either pay money, or be tried for so shameful a crime.[50]

At the Clare assizes in 1834, Inglis saw no less than forty rape cases entered; very few were actually heard, and all ended in acquittal. He wrote that

in nine cases out of ten, the crime is sworn to, merely for the purpose of getting a husband; and the plan generally succeeds.... It certainly impresses a stranger with no very favourable idea of female character, to find a girl falsely swearing a capital charge against a man whom she is willing at that moment to marry.[51]

In *Sketches of the Irish bar*, William Curran alluded wryly to this extraordinary phenomenon: 'in nine cases out of ten, it is almost impossible to divine whether the real object of the prosecutrix is the prisoner's life, or his hand and fortune.... With every step that

49 IFC Ms. Vol. 702, p. 87.
50 J. Hall, *Tour through Ireland* (2 vols., London, 1813), ii, 24.
51 Inglis, *Ireland in 1834*, p. 286.

her gentle hand conducts him towards his doom, he becomes more conjugally inclined.'[52]

Alexis de Tocqueville raised the matter in an interview with an experienced judge at the Galway assizes in 1835:

Q. I have seen on the different court calendars many 'rapes'. I have heard it said that morals are very pure. How can these two things be reconciled?

A. Morals are actually very pure. Nearly all the accusations of 'rape' are made by girls who wish in this way to force a man to marry them. If the marriage takes place the prosecution ceases, according to our laws.[53]

As to the general purity of Irish women, de Tocqueville received further confirmation from a Bishop Kinsella, who told him, 'Twenty years in the confessional have made me aware that the misconduct of girls is very rare, and that of married women is almost unknown.'[54] S.J. Connolly reports from his reading of early nineteenth-century travel writers that 'Contemporary observers in the decades preceding the famine had in general a high opinion of the sexual morals of the Irish lower orders'.[55]

Interestingly, there is no mention of the use of rape charges to secure a husband anywhere in the folklore archives. The few stories that deal with rape tell of false charges being brought against priests in order to ruin them (usually at the instigation of Protestants). Such a complete silence is remarkable when compared with the frequent mention of the topic by outside observers. The explanation may lie in a general reluctance to discuss sexual matters with folklore collectors. Stories which do involve sexual immorality usually end with a disclaimer, such as 'there was none of that round here', or 'that was a long time ago'.

52 William H. Curran, *Sketches of the Irish bar* (London, 1855), pp. 294–95.
53 Alexis de Tocqueville, *Journey in Ireland, July-August 1835* (Dublin, 1990), p. 99.
54 ibid., p. 64.
55 Connolly, *Priests and people*, p. 186.

Speculation

I have already referred to a widespread belief that bribery, perjury and 'influence' were necessary ingredients of most court victories. This could act as a deterrent for those who could not, or would not, play the game in this way; but for those who could and would, such a belief would actively encourage litigation. After all, even non-gamblers can be tempted by what seems a dead certainty. With a judge or a clerk in one's pocket, suddenly the prospect of a lawsuit becomes more appealing. Robert Kidder, in studying patterns of litigation and attitudes to law in colonial India, found that

... most literature suggests that Indians took to courts with great enthusiasm and that many became masters at manipulating them to their own ends. Much colonial correspondence concerning the courts dealt with the 'despicable' native tendency to lie, scheme, and bribe their way to court victories. Administrators took umbrage at the fact that natives treated litigation as a form of speculation and entertainment.[56]

If the evidence of foreign travellers in Ireland is to be believed, this might equally be taken as a description of legal life in the Ireland of the eighteenth and nineteenth centuries. As we have seen, Thackeray, Inglis and others portray the ordinary Irish person as being more than willing to try his or her hand at litigation over the most trivial matters; doing so with a *brio* which, it appears, was not found amongst similar classes in England.

Entertainment

Finally, it is reasonable to suspect that law for many people was, primarily, a source of gossip and entertainment. For spectators, law afforded the opportunity to watch friends, neighbours, enemies and lawyers seeking to get the better of one another in battles of wit and wisdom. One might also hope to see the downfall of some cocky lawyer or arrogant judge at the hands of an experienced witness.

---

56 Kidder, 'Toward an integrated theory of imposed law', in S. Burman and B.E. Harrell-Bond (ed.), *The imposition of law* (New York, 1979), p. 289 at p. 292.

For litigants and witnesses, it offered the chance to step into the limelight; to cross swords with supposedly better educated barristers and judges; to show off one's talent for acting, story-telling and perhaps a little creative perjury, whilst playing to a gallery of one's friends and relations. One thinks of the witness who came to the attention of John Carr while attending the sessions in Killarney in 1806. The man 'swore backwards and forwards ten times in about as many minutes, and whenever he was detected in the most abominable perjury, the auditory was thrown into convulsions of merriment'. It was Carr's opinion that many lawsuits were motivated more by a desire to show off the plaintiff's legal knowledge than by any genuine sense of grievance for a wrong done. This theme will be explored further in a later chapter.[57]

57 See below, chapter 5.

CHAPTER THREE

Tilting the scales of justice

BY AND LARGE, folk culture presents the common law as being biased in favour of the powerful – such power coming by way of class, wealth, education, achievement, religious or political affiliation. The poor man or woman entered a courtroom with the odds already stacked against them. In such circumstances, two courses of action might be followed. One would be to abandon all thought of seeking justice in the courts, and to pursue a remedy elsewhere – in arbitration, or by recourse to violent or revengeful action. The other would be to go to court, but to attempt to redress the balance by any means available. Such means might include the use of 'influence' or bribery, both of which are examined in this chapter.

INFLUENCE

Influence, while difficult to quantify, is a pervasive concept in the folk perception of the legal system – an unseen lubricant applied to the wheels of the judicial machinery. It is generally commensurate with power or status in some form, and thus the peculiar province of societal minorities – of 'them' rather than 'us'. Different examples of 'them' include Protestants, aristocrats, men of wealth, army officers, freemasons, and priests. Writing in 1818, J.C. Curwen observed that

The people in Ireland have long considered a want of interest among the higher ranks as tantamount to criminality: its influence in their opinion can control the operations of the law – can obtain pardon for the commission of the greatest crime; and no offender suffers condign punishment but the person who is destitute of powerful friends to intercede for him.[1]

1   J.C. Curwen, *Observations on the state of Ireland* (London, 1818), p. 274.

According to Sir William Wilde,

The people had long been taught that there was no law or justice for the poor man, unless his master was a magistrate, or, what would be still better, had an 'ould family grudge' with an opposing magistrate, or that the priest would interfere in his behalf.[2]

The use of influence could result in total victory; or, if the odds were too highly stacked and the perversion of justice too blatant, a significant mitigation of punishment or loss. An example of such leniency comes from Co. Kerry, where a group of men were convicted of felling trees illegally to make cudgels: 'Ba dhóbair go bhfaighidís leath-bhliain príosúin, ach thánadar [amach] ar bheagán fineála le neart *influence*.'[3]

Wherever the result of a case ran counter to popular expectation, influence was a convenient scapegoat – an explanation that covered any set of facts, without the necessity of actual proof. This is usefully illustrated by a story based on the infamous 'Wildgoose Lodge' incident, in which the burning of a huntsman's lodge near Reaghstown, Co. Louth on 30 October 1816 resulted in the deaths of eight people. According to the story, one of those charged with murder was Larry Gaynor. He was tried, convicted and sentenced to death. However, help was at hand in the shape of a man named Corbally, who stood up in court and asked the judge ' ... to give him the chance of his life for the tossing of a halfpenny. The judge must have known Corbally personally or else he was a sportsman, for he agreed to his request.'[4] Corbally won the toss, and the judge let Larry Gaynor walk out of the court a free man.

So goes the story; but in the Wildgoose Lodge affair we have one of the few instances where reliable, comprehensive historical research exists, against which the folk version may be compared. From exhaustive studies in the *Journal of the County Louth Archaeological Society*, we know firstly that twenty or so suspects

---

2   Sir William Wilde, *Irish popular superstitions* (Dublin, 1972), p. 81. *Irish popular superstitions* was first published in 1852.
3   'They should have got half a year in prison, but they came away with a small fine owing to the power of influence.' IFC Ms. Vol. 998, p. 361.
4   IFC Ms. Vol. 815, p. 169.

were returned for trial on charges of murder and arson, and that one of these was a Lawrence Gaynor. His case was heard in Dundalk on Tuesday, 31 March 1818, along with James Smith and Patrick McCullen: Smith and McCullen were found guilty and hanged, but Gaynor was acquitted.[5] Paterson, from whom we learn of Gaynor's release, does not tell us *why* he was acquitted; and given the thoroughgoing attention to detail which characterises Paterson's work, we may suppose that this is because such details were not reported in the local newspapers of the day.

It should be noted that, of the twenty-odd accused, no less than eighteen were convicted and executed. This renders Gaynor's acquittal remarkable in the extreme; and it is no surprise that, in the absence of detailed accounts of the trial, the local population evolved their own stories to explain this anomalous verdict. As to why the unlikely tale of Corbally and the coin-toss found currency, we shall never know; but the tossing of a coin is a good symbol for the view that proceedings in Irish courts of law were often far-removed from the popular sense of justice and moral right. And it offers an even chance of success, which is perhaps more than the average person could expect without powerful intervention on their behalf.

The frequency with which influence is talked of, together with documentary support for the frequency of bribery amongst the judiciary, constitute strong evidence for the reality of influence as a force within the legal system. Unfortunately, it is so easy to allege, so hard to prove, and so convenient an explanation for disliked or misunderstood decisions that it becomes impossible to gauge the true extent of its use with any degree of accuracy. All that can be done is to list the kinds of cases in which influence was said to have been used; the kinds of people whose influence was sought; and its apparent effect on the cases in question.

5   T.F.G. Paterson, 'The burning of Wildgoose Lodge', *Louth Arch Soc Jn*, xii (1950), 159, 175. For further research into the Wildgoose Lodge affair, see Daniel J. Casey, 'Wildgoose Lodge: the evidence and the lore', *Louth Arch Soc Jn*, xviii (1956), 140, and Réamonn Ó Muirí, 'The burning of Wildgoose Lodge: a selection of documents', *Louth Arch Soc Jn*, xxi (1986), 117. A fictional account of the tragedy (of dubious historical worth) can be found in Carleton's *Traits and stories of the Irish peasantry*.

Freemasons

An article in the *Irish Law Times* for 26 June 1897 referred to a case in which

a 'sub-inspector' of constabulary was tried for the murder of his 'friend' Glass, a bank clerk in Ulster. The police officer was a freemason, and, after his very proper conviction, it was commonly, though no doubt unfoundedly said, that the Irish executive would not dare have him hanged.[6]

This is a reference to a famous case from the 1870s, known as the 'Newtownstewart murder'. Thomas Hartley Montgomery was the district inspector who conducted the initial investigation into the murder; he had been a friend of the victim. At the inquest, however, it was suggested that Montgomery himself committed the crime, and he was duly arrested and charged. Three trials were held before a jury could agree on a verdict. Upon being found guilty, the prisoner made a brief speech from the dock, admitting that he had struck the fatal blow, but claiming that his mind had been 'unhinged' at the time. The issue of insanity had not been raised during the trial, and the death sentence was duly pronounced. In his summary of the case, V.T.H. Delany says that 'it was considered that if he had not made his final statement from the dock, the sentence might have been respited'.[7] It is not clear why this should have been the case: but if this was being said in legal circles, one can see how it would have given credence to the popular rumour concerning alleged masonic membership. Montgomery was hanged at Omagh gaol, but the press were excluded from the execution scene – a decision which doubtless prolonged the life of the rumour.

Belief in this form of influence seems to have been most common in Ulster, where the masonic tradition was at its strongest. A

6 *ILT & SJ*, xxxi (1897), 296. The trial formed the basis for a radio play by Denis Johnston entitled 'Murder hath no tongue [the Glass murder]', first broadcast by the B.B.C. on 7 Oct. 1937, and subsequently adapted for television. See *The dramatic works of Denis Johnston*, ed. Joseph Ronsley (3 vols, Gerrard's Cross, 1992), iii, 393.

7 V.T.H. Delany, *Christopher Palles* (Dublin, 1966), pp. 75–79.

Cavan farmer told a story concerning the murder of a young girl. A man was charged with the crime and duly convicted, but instead of being sentenced to death, he escaped with a mild gaol sentence. It was rumoured that between the time of his arrest and the trial of the offence, he had managed to become a freemason.[8] Another reputed instance of the power of the masons occurred in the case of one Beauchannon. Arrested and charged with the robbery and murder of an elderly couple, he was acquitted. 'It was said he was a freemason. He was at the funeral, and they say that when he went to carry one of the coffins the corpse started to bleed.'[9]

Throughout the county of Cavan one finds this belief in the power of freemasons to affect cases on behalf of fellow members. Magistrates in Moynalty, for instance, were said not to be anti-Catholic, but very much pro-mason: a freemason, it was said, could not be hung. A man named Fitzsimons told a folklore collector that a popular saying was, 'You needn't go to law with a man wearing the compass and square'. He went on to say that 'No man was on the Grand Jury in them days only a freemason. A lot of them would be on the common jury.... A Catholic would get on the jury if he was a freemason.'[10] A man named Lynch from neighbouring Co. Meath also heard of people asking freemasons to use their influence in law cases.[11] Another Meath man told of a particular mason who would sit on the stairs in the courtroom, thereby ensuring the magistrates could see him; he would then dictate to them the decisions they should make. McMahon said that 'If you hadn't a tendency towards freemasonry, you wouldn't get justice.... And that was the cause of so many Catholics being in the freemasons.'[12]

It is clear from that last remark that masonic power was not identical to Protestant power, but possessed (at least in the north of Ireland) a power and status independent of the religious

---

8 IFC Ms. Vol. 1197, p. 216.
9 IFC Ms. Vol. 1195, p. 367. It was widely believed that a murdered corpse would bleed in the presence of the murderer – see below, pp. 118–22.
10 IFC Ms. Vol. 1197, p. 14.
11 IFC Ms. Vol. 1197, p. 136.
12 IFC Ms. Vol. 1196, p. 229.

backgrounds of its members. Further support for this view comes from the description of a Catholic masonic leader in County Cavan named Smith, who was reputed to have considerable power over the decisions of a local judge named Curran: 'Judge Curran would do what he'd tell him ... he often influenced the judge.'[13]

Protestants

Those of the Protestant faith – the faith of the English 'oppressors' – were another class of people regarded as 'them' in matters of power. Mr Fitzsimons, quoted above in relation to the prevalence of freemasons on juries, declared that 'They'd decide in favour of a Protestant, whether he was a freemason or not'.[14] Given that judicial positions were for a long time the preserve of non-Catholics, it is hardly surprising to find a general belief that the majority of magistrates and judges were biased up until the time when Catholics began to be appointed.[15] Doctor Ryan, who according to the lore in Co. Cavan was the first Catholic magistrate to be appointed to the Baileboro district, was supposed to have called his brethren on the bench 'a bunch of bigots and a bunch of devils'. Our informant added, 'That was his honest opinion, and it was every man's honest opinion outside the ranks of the bigots and their class'. As proof, the informant offered a comparison of punishments meted out for drunkenness – whereas a Catholic would get a month in gaol, a Protestant would escape with a mere caution.[16] Another source supported this view, stating that until the turn of the century, a Catholic had virtually no chance of winning a suit against a Protestant: 'In my young days there was nothing but complaints about how the law was administered.'[17]

Another Cavan man remembered one particular incident (mentioned earlier)[18] involving one Flanagan. Having been charged with resisting arrest and with other offences relating to drunkenness,

13 IFC Ms. Vol. 1196, p. 191.
14 IFC Ms. Vol. 1197, p. 14.
15 IFC Ms. Vol. 1195, p. 380.
16 IFC Ms. Vol. 1195, p. 380.
17 IFC Ms. Vol. 1196, p. 114.
18 See above, pp. 5–6.

he was fined half a crown and released. On that same day a Catholic, who had been arrested for drunken behaviour but who had not resisted arrest, was sentenced to one month's hard labour. Our source went on to say the bigotry evident from these judgments was raised in Parliament by Joseph Biggar, and that his action prompted the introduction of Catholic magistrates into Ireland.[19] As we have seen, this latter statement is inaccurate; Catholic magistrates were operating some 40 years before Joseph Biggar's parliamentary career as MP for Co. Cavan (1874–1890) began. Biggar is an important figure in Irish folklore – a hero in the mould of O'Connell or Parnell, albeit on a smaller scale – and the fact that Clarke credited him with this achievement can be seen as another reflection of the belief, widespread it would seem in the countryside, that victories in the English legal and political system were rarely achieved without influence in higher places.

Rich and poor

Running parallel with the religious divide was the universal division between those who have, and those who have not. As far as the poor were concerned, the law was a place where, in the words of Christ, 'even the little they have shall be taken away from them':

Níor bhaol go deo d'fhear a mbeadh … an tiarna talún air fhábhar. Bhí an chúirt agus an choiste ar a gcomhairle féin acu, agus níor bheag focal uathu chun cead na gcos do scaoileadh leis an té bhris an dlí, agus bhí focal ón dtiarna ábalta ar an nduine céanna do cheangal le slabhraí i bpríosún láidir ar feadh suim gan áireamh.[20]

Ins an lá sin bhí sé de chumhacht ag tiarna talún duine [a] chuir go dtí an gcroch, ciontach nó neamhchiontach, nú duine thabhairt ón gcroich, cionntach nu neamhchionntach.[21]

---

19 IFC Ms. Vol. 1196, p. 165.
20 'The man with the landlord on his side need never fear. They had the court and the jury under their control, and it only took a word from them to free the man who broke the law; and a word from the landlord could chain the same person in a strong prison for an unlimited period.' IFC Ms. Vol. 41, p. 366.
21 'In those days the landlord had power to send someone to the gallows, guilty or not guilty, or to free them from it, guilty or not guilty.' IFC Ms. Vol. 39, p. 54.

The latter statement is preceded by a story told of Daniel O'Connell which clearly illustrates the belief that separate laws existed for rich and poor. On a particular day in court, two men were convicted of a vicious form of assault known as *cardáil* – to wit, taking a steel comb used for carding wool, and dragging it down the victim's back – and were duly sentenced to death. That same day, a 'gentleman' was convicted of burning his house down in order to collect the value of its insurance – a crime which, according to the storyteller, also carried the penalty of death. The judge was about to let the gentleman go free, before O'Connell intervened. Pointing out the hypocrisy and injustice at work in the two contrasting judgments, he accused the rich man of having committed a worse crime than the other two and threatened to raise the matter in Parliament. Faced with this unappealing prospect, the judge donned his black cap once more and sentenced the rich man to the same fate as the peasants.

From Limerick comes a story of a man named Quinlan, who served in the British army for eleven years under a Colonel Barrington – even saving his life on one occasion 'when a soldier in the Sikh war in the Punjab'. Shortly after his return to Ireland, Quinlan met a newly evicted widow. Angry at the fate which had befallen her, he met and shot the land agent responsible. Quinlan was arrested, tried, convicted and sentenced to death. Fortunately for him, he had a powerful ally in the colonel whose life he had once saved. Barrington pleaded Quinlan's case before the lord lieutenant, and at length secured a commutation of the sentence from death to transportation.[22]

The prejudice of the legal system in favour of the landed classes was so pronounced, according to rural tradition, that the only way for a poor person to secure justice was to find someone equally influential to take up their case. One of the most infamous cases of the nineteenth century was that of the *Cailín Bán* murder – the abduction and subsequent killing of a young Limerick girl, upon which Gerald Griffin based his novel, *The collegians*. The murder was found to have been committed by one Sullivan, on

22 IFC Ms. Vol. 1193, p. 331; Vol. 1194, p. 307. The latter account dates the story at around 1900.

the orders of his master, John Scanlon, a local squire's son. Despite the considerable influence of his family, and the skilful defending of Daniel O'Connell, Scanlon was convicted and hanged. We are told that 'The people believe that only for the active part the Knight of Glin and other landlords took in the prosecution of the case Scanlon might have got off free'.[23] This popular cynicism about the power of law where the rich were concerned finds an echo in a letter from Daniel O'Connell to his wife, written on 15 March 1820 – the day after the Scanlon trial had concluded. He wrote:

... This is a good assizes. You will, however, be surprised to hear that I had a client convicted yesterday for a murder for whom I fought a hard battle, and yet I do not feel any the most slight regret at his conviction. It is very unusual with me to be *so* satisfied, but he is a horrid villain.... He will be hanged tomorrow unless being a gentleman prevents him.[24]

This last sentence may be a throwaway remark on O'Connell's part, but it does reflect what many of his fellow countrymen believed – that there was a different law for the rich. To their way of thinking, the undoing of John Scanlon was not his conviction, but his abandonment by the ruling gentry. The horrific nature of his crime and its nationwide notoriety had made it impossible for the aristocracy to support him. Without their protection, he was doomed, as any ordinary man would have been.

Power to save from hanging

Mention of the death penalty brings us to consider a special area of influence: the alleged power of certain individuals to save people from hanging. Some stories imply a power of absolute pardon, others are silent on whether freedom or mere commutation of sentence was in issue. An account from Kerry mentions one Admiral Moriarty, who reputedly 'had the power of bringing three men from the gallows'.[25] Another tale involving the admiral stated that three a year could be saved, and that the power passed

---

23 IFC Ms. Vol. 1193, p. 336.
24 Maurice O'Connell (ed.), *The correspondence of Daniel O'Connell* (8 vols., Dublin, 1972–80), ii, 243.
25 IFC Ms. Vol. 1167, p. 186.

to his wife on his death.[26] A third source suggests that more than three could be saved, and places the admiral's own death at around 1844.[27] Regrettably, we are left completely in the dark as to the origin of this gift, and why and how it was bestowed.

In the case of a renowned *gaiscíoch* (warrior-hero) named Mac Finghín Dubh, we are told how he came by a similar power. The story goes that the son of the king of England came to stay with him for a week or so, and at the end of that time, offered Mac Finghín Dubh any boon he craved. The hero chose the right to save three people from the gallows each year.[28]

In Co. Mayo, a landlord named Donnchadh Bingham was reputed to have the power to save a man from hanging at any time of year, although the storyteller added that the power was never used.[29] A Kerry woman who also never used her power of clemency was Bess Rice.[30] As with Bingham and Mac Finghín Dubh, there is no even approximate indication of when Bess Rice lived.

Moving to Galway, we are told that a Captain O'Mara had the power to save from hanging, but no details are given, except for a story in which he uses it to secure freedom and pardon for one of his tenants, who had been convicted of some unnamed crime and sentenced to death at Galway town court. Interestingly, we are told that the captain lived not in Galway, but in Co. Clare.[31] The magic number three crops up again in a Corkman's reference to a powerful family he calls 'na Barraigh', who could and did save that number of people from the gallows annually.[32] Perhaps this is a reference to the Barron family, or 'na Barúnaigh' as Pádraig Breathnach from neighbouring Co. Waterford calls them: he says initially that this family could save *two* a year from hanging, but then tells a story in which three are freed – admittedly in unusual circumstances. The three in question were two brothers and their

26 IFC Ms. Vol. 700, p. 451.
27 IFC Ms. Vol. 936, p. 495.
28 IFC Ms. Vol. 1167, p. 581. In another version, the right is restricted to one person per year: IFC Ms. Vol. 698, p. 445.
29 IFC Ms. Vol. 708, p. 44.
30 IFC Ms. Vol. 702, p. 424.
31 IFC Ms. Vol. 627, p. 531.
32 IFC Ms. Vol. 643, p. 92.

step-brother. The mother was asked by Barron to choose one to be saved; she chose the step-son, because he 'had no-one but himself'. Barron was impressed with this gesture, and ordered that all three be freed.[33] Finally, a Cavan farmer told a folk collector, 'I always heard that a freemason could save a life every year from the gallows.'[34]

Court officials

An interesting sub-genre of those with power to affect judicial decisions were the clerks, criers, ushers and other minor officials who populated the ordinary courts of the land. Thackeray encountered such a man at the Waterford assizes. He wrote of

... the great coolness with which a fellow who seemed a sort of clerk, usher, and Irish interpreter to the court, recommended a prisoner, who was making rather a long defence, to be quiet. I asked why the man might not have his say. 'Sure', says he, 'he's said all he has to say, and there's no use in any more'; but there was no use in attempting to convince Mr Usher that the prisoner was the best judge on this point; in fact the poor devil shut his mouth at the admonition, and was found guilty with perfect justice.[35]

A judge who appears a number of times in Maurice Healy's reminiscences of the Munster circuit is William O'Brien,[36] who on his death was the subject of fulsome tributes to his learning, erudition, charity and sense of honour from bench and bar alike.[37] His reputation amongst ordinary Irish people was rather less glorious, and Healy attributes this in no small measure to O'Brien's relationship with his crier[38], a man named Ford:

33 IFC Ms Vol. 33, p. 83.
34 IFC Ms. Vol. 1197, p. 71.
35 Thackeray, *The Irish sketchbook*, p. 52.
36 Born 1832; appointed judge of Common Pleas Division 1882; transferred to Queen's Bench Division 1883; became a privy councillor 1890; died 1899.
37 See for example *ILT & SJ*, xxxiii (1899), 518.
38 Those unfamiliar with the post of court crier might take note of Gerald Griffin's description in one of his *Munster tales* (New York, 1979), Vol. 2, pp. 207–08:
    ... the crier, a bustling and important personage whose duty it is in Irish courts to be as noisy as possible in procuring 'silence'; to perform the

It was no uncommon thing to see Ford whispering in the Judge's ear, to the latter's accompaniment of: 'Oh-h! Oh-h! God bless my soul! What a ruffian!' soon to be followed by a sentence of extreme severity. Sometimes Ford's good offices would be invoked on behalf of a prisoner; then the Judge would address the Crown Prosecutor: 'Misther Adams; Misther Adams; I think this young man has been led asthray. He is a very foolish young man; is there nobody who will be answerable for him?' Promptly there would be observed shining upon the court from a back seat the countenance of some jolly son of Bacchus, whose name would not carry much weight in any bank or counting-house – 'I will, me Lord!' 'Oh-h! Oh-h! And who is this respectable gentleman that has so charitably come forward? Come down here, sir; I'm much obliged to you. Prisoner, you should be very grateful to this worthy gentleman, who is saving you from the disgrace of prison. Let him be bound over, Misther O'Grady; and he may go.'[39]

Healy goes on to tell a story[40] told to him by his father (a well-known solicitor in his day), in which Ford's influence nearly produced a serious miscarriage of justice. A man called Sheehan had been courting the sister of a man named Brown. As the Browns were poor, the match was strongly opposed by Sheehan's mother, sister and brother, who all lived on Sheehan's own small farm. At length, it was said that Sheehan had persuaded his family to emigrate to New Zealand, with himself and his bride to follow them in due course. After some time, however, it was found that the family had never left Ireland, but had in fact been murdered and buried on the Sheehan farm. Sheehan was charged with murder, tried, convicted and hanged; but it was felt that he must have had an accomplice. Suspicion fell on Brown, and he was arraigned for trial. Brown had an alibi, and a number of witnesses willing to attest to it; nonetheless, defence counsel (Richard Adams and D.B. Sullivan) were unsure before the trial whether to

part of mouth-piece to the clerk of the crown – marshall the spectators to their different places – thrust out the orange-women – knock little boys on the head with a long white wand – and convey by means of a slit in the end of said wand, epistles from all quarters of the court.
Munster tales was first published in 1827.
39 Healy, *The old Munster circuit*, p. 12.
40 ibid., pp. 19–24.

call any evidence, or simply to rely on attacking the weaknesses of the prosecution case.

The trial proceeded without a decision having been made. At the conclusion of the Crown case, however, the defence decided that the calling of witnesses to support the prisoner's version of events would be necessary. Then, just before the court was about to resume,

... the door of the Judge's room opened, and Ford, the crier, came out with a purposeful air. Moving along the other side of the table, he halted in front of Adams, and, leaning forward, he said in a tense and meaning whisper: 'Mr Adams; *call no evidence in this case!*' Adams stiffened: 'What do you mean?' he asked. 'Mark my words,' said Ford solemnly; 'call no evidence!' And as he said these words a second time, the door opened again and the judge returned to Court.[41]

This mysterious announcement from Ford threw Adams and his team into confusion, and they asked the judge for a further short adjournment, in order to consider their next actions. This was granted, but Ford left the courtroom with the judge, leaving them none the wiser. In the end, the strange warning was taken as a hint that the judge was not at all convinced by the prosecution case, and it was decided to call no evidence.

The court resumed, and, the judge having been informed of this decision, counsel for both sides were invited to sum up. The judge then began his charge to the jury:

'Gentlemen of the Jury,' he said in his most impressive tones, 'you have listened with careful attention to the speech of Mr Adams, and you now know full well, even if you had not known it before, the exact case which the prisoner desires to be presented on his behalf. Gentlemen, it will, no doubt, have occurred to you as it has occurred to me, not once but many times, that if there were one word of truth in that story, there must be sitting in this Court or within easy summons of it a large number of persons who could have gone into that witness-box to swear to its genuineness; and *not one witness has been called for the defence!*'

Adams gave a cry and collapsed ... all through that terrible charge to the jury the unfortunate defending counsel were as though possessed;

41 ibid., p. 22.

and when the jury and the judge had retired to their respective rooms, Adams began to rave like a man demented. He must see the judge; he must rush to Dublin and see the Lord Lieutenant; he must cross to London and see the Queen.[42]

In the event, his fears were unfounded; the jury disregarded the judge's hints and quickly returned a verdict of 'not guilty'. After sitting alone in the empty courtroom for some time, with his head in his hands, Adams rose and made for the bar-room. On his way there, he encountered Ford once more:

Adams gave a yell and sprang at his throat; the terrified Ford screamed for help. 'For God's sake, Mr Adams; for the love of God, leave go of my throat, you're choking me.' 'You ruffian!' roared Adams; 'you infernal blackguard! What did you mean by telling me to call no evidence,' and he slackened his grip to enable Ford to reply. 'Mean?' cried Ford. 'Mean? Sure, Mr Adams, you know well that I can't abide perjury!'[43]

In Carleton's novel of the Great Famine, *The black prophet*, chapter fourteen gives a description of one Dick-o'-the-Grange, a 'middleman magistrate of the old school', and it is worth quoting as much for the picture of how justice was administered as for Carleton's comments on the nature of Dick's relationship with his clerk, one Jemmy Branigan:

Dick-o'-the-Grange held his office, as many Irish magistrates have done before him, in his own parlour; that is to say, he sat in an armchair at one of the windows which was thrown open for him, whilst those who came to seek justice, or, as they termed it, law, at his hands, were compelled to stand uncovered on the outside, no matter whether the weather was stormy or otherwise. We are not now about to pronounce any opinion upon the constitutional spirit of Dick's decisions, inasmuch as nineteen out of every twenty of them were come to by the only 'Magistrates Guide' he ever was acquainted with – to wit, the redoubtable Jemmy Branigan. Jemmy was his clerk, and although he could neither read nor write, yet in cases where his judgments did not give satisfaction,

---

42 ibid., p. 23.
43 ibid., p. 24. Richard Adams later became a County Court judge, and is the subject of numerous folk stories in that capacity: see below, pp. 65–70.

he was both able and willing to *set his mark* upon the discontented parties, in a fashion that did not allow his blessed signature to be easily forgotten.[44]

BRIBERY

The level of bribery in the Irish legal system of the eighteenth, nineteenth and early twentieth centuries is well-nigh impossible to assess. That it did exist is plain – one might be tempted to infer that simply from the nature of mankind. If more positive proof is required, one could turn to Henry Inglis. In 1834, he stated his opinion that 'the substitution of a stipendiary, for an unpaid magistracy, is essential to the peace of Ireland'. His reasoning was that an unpaid magistrate was more likely to succumb to the temptation of accepting bribes in one form or another; in particular, he noted the widespread practice of magistrates turning a blind eye to faction fights, on foot of some personal service being rendered to them by members of the participating clans.[45] Travelling around Ireland in 1822, Thomas Reid wrote that he knew magistrates in Ireland 'to whom any man might send a "compliment" with as little ceremony as he would for a pound of tea to a grocer's shop and with as little chance of offending'.[46] Such a magistrate is referred to by Waldron in his book on the Maamtrasna murders – one Joseph Blake of Carrick Lodge, Cornamona: 'a colourful character, nicknamed "Joeen na gCoileach" for his partiality to well-fed cocks. (A plump bird on the eve of the Assizes in Clonbur, when he acted as a magistrate, was known to work wonders in the courtroom on the morrow).'[47]

Maurice Healy relates a further anecdote concerning Judge William O'Brien which hints at bribery. While the evidence is not conclusive, the story serves well as an illustration of the type of thing that might fuel popular perceptions of the law as being mired in corruption. The case involved a young member of one of Cork's wealthier families, who had been accused of cheating at cards in the Cork Club. Several eye-witnesses attested to the truth

44 Carleton, *The black prophet*, ch.14.
45 Inglis, *Ireland in 1834*, p. 286.
46 Reid, *Travels in Ireland* (London, 1823), p. 370.
47 Waldron, *Maamtrasna*, p. 53.

of the accusation, which seemed irrefutable. However, when the case came on for hearing, Judge O'Brien allowed defending counsel to effectively 'laugh the case out of court', through mimicking and satirising the witnesses.

The case dissolved in laughter; a tremendous triumph for the brilliant advocate who had conducted it for the plaintiff. But to laugh a case out of court is the hardest of all things to do, and cannot be done at all if the presiding Judge does not give his blessing to the process. And, whatever may have been the merits of the case, the reputation of the Bench was not improved when Mr Justice O'Brien subsequently accepted from the proud and happy mother of the plaintiff the gift of a handsome residence at Douglas, outside the city of Cork.

In a footnote, Healy adds that he was told that the actual reason for this donation was the existence of a bond of service between O'Brien's father and the donor's family. But, as he points out, that was not how the public chose to explain the gift.[48]

The folklore archive contains numerous stories of bribes being offered, in which they are, on the whole, accepted. Only two sources indicated that bribery was viewed with any level of distaste by the common people – one saying that it was 'on nearly the same basis as perjury' (although not as frequently resorted to),[49] and the other saying that it was regarded as dishonest – 'a bribe buys your reputation'.[50] This is not necessarily to say that theirs was a minority opinion: it may be that others were not asked what the people thought of bribery, or simply took it as self-evident that such behaviour would not find favour with the majority of 'decent' people.

Bribes could take different forms. Mr Gibson, a magistrate in the Cavan / Meath area, was persuaded to act leniently towards two boys accused of assaulting a policeman, when their mother bought a pair of boots from Gibson's shop;[51] the support of a Cork judge was secured through a present of a goat;[52] a landlord

48 Healy, *The old Munster circuit*, pp. 24–26.
49 IFC Ms. Vol. 1196, p. 100.
50 IFC Ms. Vol. 1195, p. 399.
51 IFC Ms. Vol. 1195, p. 410.
52 IFC Ms. Vol. 1003, p. 385.

in Co. Clare accepted an offer, again from the mother of some boys in trouble – this time for faction fighting – to have his horses fed with oats. He was said to have promised in return: 'Beidh aithint ag mo chuid capaill ort lá na cúirte.'[53] In another Clare story, a man bribed a justice with a calf; watching as the case proceeded in his favour, the man exclaimed in the court: 'Is deas mar a labhrann mo gamhainín ins an gcúirt seo inniu.'[54]

In a dispute between two branches of the Butler family over land boundaries, we are told that the engineer enlisted to give expert evidence was bribed, although we are not told what with.[55] In one of the tales of Daniel O'Connell, he is defending a Catholic who has been charged with some crime by a Protestant. The Protestant bribes the judge with wine to ensure a conviction. O'Connell, on discovering this, instructs his Catholic client to send the judge a mare as a counterbalancing 'gift'. This is done. During the hearing of the case, O'Connell pretends to fall asleep. On 'waking', he declares that he had been dreaming of a mare drowning in wine! The judge realises that O'Connell is aware of the bribes, and lets the defendant go free.[56]

A story of a Kerry poacher also has slight sectarian overtones. The man was caught by two gamekeepers, one of whom he injured in the resulting scuffle. The case against him was to be tried by two judges: one an English Protestant, the other an Irish Catholic. The accused brought two sheep to offer them, '... féachaint an ndéanfaidís aon *fair play* a thabhairt dó nuair a bhí an maor a' dearbhú chomh dian air.'[57] The English judge refused the bribe; however, his Irish colleague accepted one of the sheep. He promised to do his best for the poacher in court, on condition that, if successful, the poacher would give him the other sheep also.

Finally, a story supposedly told by O'Connell himself illustrates how one Denis O'Brien turned a judge's susceptibility to bribery to his advantage, without it costing him a penny:

53 'My horses will recognise you on the day of court.' IFC Ms. Vol. 41, p. 368.
54 'My calf is speaking nicely in this court today.' IFC Ms. Vol. 38, p. 219.
55 IFC Ms. Vol. 354, p. 374.
56 Uí Ógáin, *Immortal Dan*, p. 135.
57 '... to see if they would offer him any fair play when the warden was swearing so hard against him.' IFC Ms. Vol. 692, p. 558.

Denis O'Brien had a record at Nenagh – the judge talked of purchasing a pair of carriage horses, and Denis accordingly sent him a magnificent pair, hoping they would answer his Lordship, &c. The judge graciously accepted the horses and praised their points extravagantly, and, what was more important for Denis, he charged the jury in his favour, and obtained a verdict for him. The instant Denis gained his point he sent in a bill to the judge for the full value of the horses. His Lordship called Denis aside to expostulate privately with him. 'Oh, Mr O'Brien,' said he, 'I did not think you meant to charge me for those horses. Come, now, my dear friend, why should I pay you for them?' 'Upon my word, that's curious talk,' retorted Denis, in a tone of defiance ; 'I'd like to know why your Lordship should not pay me for them?' To this inquiry, of course, a reply was impossible; all the judge had for it was to hold his peace and pay the money.[58]

Other targets of bribery include witnesses,[59] bailiffs,[60] and a court crier – who, despite the inducement of a bottle of whiskey from one of the parties to a civil suit, could not manage to secure the desired decision from the judge.[61]

58 *ILT & SJ*, xxxi (1897), 364.
59 IFC Ms. Vol. 1197, p. 76.
60 IFC Ms. Vol. 1197, p. 268.
61 IFC Ms. Vol. 1196, p. 70.

CHAPTER FOUR

The personnel of the courts

HUMAN BEINGS LIVE on the cusp of abstraction and sensation: that is, our comprehension of the world around us is based partly on what we experience directly through our physical senses, and partly on abstract conceptions of that which we have not yet, or can not physically perceive. Traditional jurisprudence, in its definition of law, elevates the abstract at the expense of the physical. In considering law as a universal phenomenon, it is thought best to ignore the details of how it is actually implemented and received by real people. Kelsen's Pure Theory of Law, which 'endeavours to free the science of law from all foreign elements',[1] is perhaps the *reductio ad absurdum* of this approach.

Sociological jurisprudence, in contrast, embraces the local and the personal in its search for the true meaning of law. It recognises that our conceptions of what law is and does, and our judgments as to its moral and societal worth, can be strongly affected by our actual experiences at the hands of the legal system. This is particularly true of the less well-educated groups in society, and it is as well to bear that in mind when considering general statements on the subject which surface in the folklore archives. For instance, in a previous chapter, we referred to a number of sayings warning people to steer clear of involvement with the law.[2] A number of general reasons which might have prompted these sayings were proffered; but it is also possible that the sayings are not really general at all. They may have been the peculiar response of one village or town to a harsh or biased judge who presided there at one time.

This distinction between what is of general import and what is purely local should be remembered as we look at what the average Irish person thought of the personnel that make up the

---

1 Hans Kelsen, 'The pure theory of law: its method and fundamental concepts', *LQR*, 1 (1934), 474, 477.
2 See above, pp. 24–25.

legal system – of judges, justices, magistrates, barristers, solicitors, minor court officers, bailiffs, revenue officers, process-servers and the like. Given the inherent weaknesses of folk material as an historical source, it may not be possible to draw exact lines between general belief and local tradition; but the value of any analysis on which we embark will be increased if we remember to approach all general statements with a degree of caution.

JUDGES, JUSTICES, MAGISTRATES

In actual fact, there are few enough references to the judiciary as a whole in the folklore archives: most stories are concerned with specific judges, or even specific decisions. However, some Kerry sources criticised stipendiary magistrates as a group: 'Bhíodar sár-thugtha do fineáil throm agus priosún fada a thabhairt mar bhreith i gcursaí suaracha.'[3] As we have seen, allegations of prejudice were most common in the north of Ireland, where the Protestant/Catholic conflict and the strength of freemasonry fuelled peasant suspicions. A Cavan farmer named Soden said that there was 'very good law' in the English courts, except where a Catholic was going up against either a Protestant or a freemason.[4] Another Cavan source said that some unionist magistrates were fair, despite being generally disliked: on the other hand, nationalist magistrates were seen as being lenient towards everyone.[5] Mr Soden's opinion reflects the conclusions of R.B. McDowell in his study of the Irish court system in the nineteenth century. According to McDowell, allegations of incompetence dropped off sharply following a series of petty sessions reforms: 'From about 1830, when justices of the peace were attacked, it was usually not on the grounds of incompetence but for alleged displays of political bias.'[6]

---

3 'They were extremely fond of giving heavy fines and long prison sentences for trivial matters.' IFC Ms. Vol. 1125, p. 78; Vol. 1195, p. 379.
4 IFC Ms. Vol. 1197, p. 216.
5 IFC Ms. Vol. 1196, p. 45.
6 McDowell, 'The Irish courts of law', *IHS*, x (1957), 363, 372.

Leniency / compassion

Turning to the tales of individual judges, we find that stories of kind, lenient judges outnumber those of biased or severe ones. Perhaps this indicates that severity was the rule, and that any deviation from this was remarkable enough to stick in the folk memory. Of course, it could equally be taken at face value, as evidence that most judges were regarded favourably by the Irish peasantry. One interesting example of a justice to whom respect was accorded comes from de Latocnaye, writing around 1796. When in Killarney with a local justice of the peace named Mr Herbert, he witnessed a fight break out in the midst of a funeral procession. Mr Herbert acted immediately, breaking up the fight and then hearing arguments from both sides. It turned out that the fight was between the husband of the dead woman and her brother, over where she should be buried. Mr Herbert, having heard both sides, decided that the husband had the right to choose the burying-place; and there the matter rested. De Latocnaye recorded his astonishment at how quickly and easily the magistrate had managed to impose his authority on the scene, saying: 'I must say I imagined that the combatants would unite to tear him to pieces, as a stranger meddling with things which did not belong to him.... [But] the peasants showed the greatest respect to the magistrate, and submitted promptly to his decision.'[7]

From Kerry comes a story of a man charged with stealing horses. The day before the hearing, the accused met a well-dressed man in the street. They fell into conversation, during the course of which the accused man admitted to the stranger that he did in fact steal the horses. He then invited his new acquaintance to join him for a drink. The well-dressed man refused, and they parted company. The next day, in court, it transpired that the judge was none other than the same well-dressed man. The thief,

7 Le chevalier de Latocnaye, *A Frenchman's walk through Ireland, 1796–97* (Belfast, 1984), p. 106. De Latocnaye (real name Jacques Louis de Bougrenet) was forced to emigrate from Brittany during the French Revolution. He settled in London in 1793. In 1796, he began a walking tour of Ireland: the subsequent self-published account of his adventures was well received by the reading public. Notwithstanding its light-hearted style, it is a useful snapshot of contemporary society as it appeared to a young outsider. De Latocnaye's text was first published in French in 1797, and in English in 1917.

having already confessed to him, took fright – yelling and shaking his hands at the bench: the judge, however, said nothing of what had passed between them the previous day. Instead, he ordered the hysterical thief to be removed from court and released, on the basis that he was mad. The storyteller tells us that the judge regarded the thief as a 'worthy' man (*fiúntach*) because he had offered to buy him a drink.[8]

A Kerry magistrate named Ó Gearaíl was travelling home one evening, when one of the wheels came off his buggy. A man named Tom Sullivan, who lived in a nearby house, came out and fixed it, allowing the magistrate to complete his journey that night. Some time later, Tom became involved in a brawl with a peeler who had been insulting the local Land League, and ended up stabbing the unfortunate policeman with a knife. Tom was arrested and brought before Ó Gearaíl, who duly released him on the grounds of there being no doctor to certify that the peeler was in danger. The story concluded with a happy ending: 'Ní misde dhuit a rá nár tarraingíodh trí chúirt ná trí chaibidil riamh ó shin é.'[9]

Another example of leniency appears in a tale concerning the wreck of a man-o-war ship, 'The Magpie', off the coast of Clare in April 1864. As the debris washed ashore, the local populace commenced their own ad hoc 'salvage' operation – taking copper and brass fittings, nails, bolts and barrels of meat from under the noses of the still-sleeping coastguards. The ship's captain managed to catch one unfortunate individual with a meat barrel, and promptly sentenced him to death. The crowd were horrified, but a judge intervened and ordered that the man be set free immediately: 'Dúirt sé go mba raic na rudaí a bhíodar á thógáil, agus ná raibh aon dlí leis.'[10] The story as told leaves a number of intriguing gaps; one would have liked to have asked the storyteller under what authority the captain passed the original death sentence, and how and why the judge intervened to overturn it.

---

8 IFC Ms. Vol. 78, p. 101.

9 'It need not be said that he [Tom] was never again brought before a court or tribunal.' IFC Ms. Vol. 1147, p. 472.

10 'He said that the things they were taking were wreckage, and that there was no law against it.' IFC Ms. Vol. 38, p. 29.

What is clear, though, is that the judge is seen as being on the side of the people.

One could also see this story as a triumph of custom over 'lawyer's law'. As John Rule has pointed out, popular ideas of what constituted salvage were often strongly divergent from the official, legal position.[11] The importance of wrecks to the poor living on the coasts of Ireland and Britain was considerable. Aside from the cargoes being carried, the very planks, ropes, nuts and bolts with which a ship was constructed could all be put to good use. Customary rights of salvage were of enormous importance to coastal dwellers, as witnessed by the fact that attempts to exercise them could often be accompanied by violence. An example of this occurred at Clonderlaw Bay in Ireland, in 1811. The crew of an American vessel (and some local yeomanry sent to defend her) were subjected to sustained musket-fire over a three-hour period from between two and three hundred locals, wishing to take possession of the ship.[12] Taking all this into account, it can be supposed that a judge who gave a decision favouring the locals in a salvage dispute, as the judge in the 'Magpie' case was said to have done, would be granted a special status in the popular tradition.

In Limerick, a magistrate named Galway made himself popular by the manner in which he dealt with the case of a man named Burns – a local 'hero' who had beaten and humiliated a recently appointed District Inspector. Galway made use of every opportunity in court to further mock and insult the unfortunate officer. The case ended with Burns being fined 10 shillings – but the judge then paid the fine himself: 'He considered it well worth his while to pull the feathers from the D.I.'[13]

A Connemara tale introduces a 'gentleman' (*duine uasal*) named Seoirse Muilleoir, who plays a somewhat ambiguous role in the ensuing story. A young man was charged with houghing cattle,[14] on

---

11 John G. Rule, 'Wrecking and coastal plunder', in Douglas Hay et al. (ed.), *Albion's fatal tree: crime and society in eighteenth-century England* (London, 1975), p. 172.

12 *Annual Register*, liii (1811), 4, 114.

13 IFC Ms. Vol. 1194, p. 550.

14 'Houghing' refers to the malicious wounding of livestock, often by severing leg muscles, and was a common practice of agrarian secret societies during agitation over land.

the false evidence of an enemy. The case was heard by Seoirse. After the informer had given evidence, Seoirse accused him of having been bribed to swear against the defendant; he then released the young man, and ordered the informer to pay all costs.

From events as told, there seems little doubt that Seoirse was a justice or magistrate of some sort; yet he is referred to by the storyteller as 'an t-ard chomhairleach ins an cúirt' – that is, the chief counsellor in the court. Furthermore, in a song written in his honour, Seoirse is clearly expected to be, in effect, an advocate for one side:

... tógfaidh sé mo pháirt agus is láidir é m'*action*
Is é an t-ard chomhairleach i dteach na cúirte é
tabharfaidh sé mise abhaile.[15]

Perhaps some of this confusion was rooted in the fact that barristers in Ireland could act as justices in certain circumstances. In 1787, a new breed of judge was created to assist the justices at quarter sessions. Chosen from the ranks of the bar, they were called 'assistant barristers'. Over the next 90 years or so, their jurisdiction was periodically increased.[16] In 1877, they were given the new title of 'county court judge', but doubtless the name 'barrister' or 'assistant barrister' would have continued in collo-quial use for some time after that. A man from Cavan told a collector that 'The name that most people had for a county court judge was "the barrister". That was because they were barristers before they got to be judges.'[17] Of course, barristers could also be

---

15 'He'll take my part and my action is strong / He's the chief counsellor in the courthouse / He'll bring me home.' IFC Ms. Vol. 866, p. 134.
16 See generally W.N. Osborough, 'The Irish legal system, 1796–1877', in Caroline Costello (ed.), *The Four Courts: 200 years* (Dublin, 1996), p. 33 and R.B. McDowell, 'The Irish courts of law, 1801–1914', *IHS*, x (1957), 363. John Carr saw a barrister presiding over Quarter Sessions in Killarney in 1806: he wrote that '... justice was expeditiously and I believe substantially administered by the barrister, who is addressed by that name, and who appeared to be perfectly competent to the discharge of his judicial duties.... Instead of counsel, solicitors pleaded.' (*The stranger in Ireland*, pp. 377–78.) See also J.C. Curwen, *Observations on the state of Ireland* (London, 1818), p. 273.
17 IFC Ms. Vol. 1196, p. 484.

appointed to act as justices of the peace. In those circumstances, a barrister who, after many years, became a justice of the peace might still be known locally as 'the barrister' despite his new judicial status.

A kind judge is the subject of another song, this time from county Cavan, called 'The Widow's Son'. The song was prefaced in the folk archives with the following introduction: 'They say that in olden times it wasn't an uncommon thing for a mother to go down on her knees in the Court and make a plea to the judge to not send her son to gaol. And if the judge was tender-hearted, he'd grant her wishes.' The words of the chorus contain this particular widow's plea:

Don't send my boy to prison, for the thought would drive me mad
Remember, I'm a poor widow, and I'm pleading for my lad.

The song ends with the judge releasing the son with an admonition to behave from then on in a manner worthy of his mother's love.[18] Another successful plea to a judge's heartstrings is found in a Clare tale. A man was convicted of murdering his wife, having struck her in a fit of rage. Before the judge donned the black cap to pronounce a sentence of death, the doomed man was given leave to address the court. He proceeded to read out a poem he had written, praising the beauty of his young wife, and lamenting her death. The judge, greatly affected by this display of remorseful, tortured love, ordered that the man be set free.[19]

Humour

It seems that a sense of humour was a valued attribute amongst the rural populace, and a number of stories involve justices and magistrates who are willing to grant a pardon for the price of a good laugh. In one such, the accused, a poor man, was captain of a small seine-boat.[20] In court, a gentleman named Mac Finghín

18 IFC Ms. Vol. 1196, p. 489.
19 IFC Ms. Vol. 38, p. 276.
20 A seine-boat is a boat adapted for carrying and throwing out a seine – a fishing net designed to hang vertically in the water, the ends being drawn together to enclose the fish.

Dubh (a man of some power and influence, who is portrayed in this and other stories as being on the side of the underprivileged)[21] took a seat beside the judge. When the accused man entered, Mac Finghín Dubh greeted him cordially, referring to him as 'captain'. Surprised, the judge asked the accused what army he was in: when the man explained that he wasn't in the army, and was merely the captain of his own small fishing boat, the judge laughed, and at Mac Fhingín Dubh's request, let him go.[22]

Humour also worked for a character named Meehan, who was constantly being arrested for drunkenness. On one occasion, irritated by this recurring misbehaviour, the magistrate said to him, 'I'll give you Dundalk' – meaning imprisonment in Dundalk gaol. Came the quick reply, 'Well, your honour, I'd be glad of a house in it.' Amused by Meehan's answer, the magistrate released him without even exacting a fine.[23]

Some time around 1840, a Kerryman named Florence O'Sullivan travelled to Cork city on a mare. He was arrested for drunkenness, brought before the mayor's court, and sentenced to gaol. On receiving the sentence, Florence went over to his mare, patted it, and said: 'Cheer up horse; don't despair / You'll be a horse when he's no mayor.' The mayor appreciated the wit, and revoked the sentence.[24]

Judge Adams

Numerous stories from the Tipperary / Limerick area concern a judge named Adams.[25] We are told that he worked on a news-

21 See above, p. 49.
22 IFC Ms. Vol. 27, p. 146.
23 IFC Ms. Vol. 1196, p. 1. Other stories of witty drunkards are at Vol. 983, p. 50; and Vol. 696, p. 75.
24 IFC Ms. Vol. 696, pp. 74–75. Florence 'Silver Tongue' O'Sullivan was a well known poet and hedge schoolmaster from south Kerry.
25 Most likely a reference to Richard Adams, a celebrated barrister on the Munster Circuit (see above, pp. 51–53) who later became a County Court judge for the Limerick area. Serjeant A.M. Sullivan penned the following description of him (*The last serjeant*, p. 50):
> Of all the County Courts, that presided over by Richard Adams, who became Judge of the County of Limerick, was the most remarkable. What might happen in it at any moment of any day was beyond the wit of man to forecast. At times the proceedings were those of a wise and shrewd tribunal, at times they were a pantomime in which the rules even of

paper before 'going for law'.[26] He seems to have been especially popular with the local people. Whilst some of the stories told of him may not be true, or may in fact have involved a different judge, when taken together they paint an interesting portrait of the type of man he was believed to be. From this we may make some tentative conclusions as to the qualities which gained a judge respect in the popular mind.

In the first place, he was esteemed for the down-to-earth, common-sense nature of his judgments. We are told that he 'believed a man in his position should rely on common-sense in his interpretation of the rules of the law.'[27] The example was given of a challenge to the validity of a woman's will, in which she had left all her estate to her nephew. No less than 46 relatives combined to bring the action, alleging that she had lacked mental capacity. The testatrix had been well known during her lifetime for eccentric behaviour; nonetheless, Adams allowed the will to stand, for the simple reason that to divide her small property between 46 people would be impractical and would serve no useful purpose. We are told that 'this decision pleased the general public.'[28] In family disputes, he strongly urged the parties to settle out of court, and would often adjourn cases to enable them to do so. In disputes over boundaries between property, he usually visited the sites himself, rather than relying on witness testimony.[29]

---

decency were not strictly observed. No man knew and understood the Munster peasant as well as Adams. No judicial decisions of any tribunal were so consistently right in effect or so wrong in delivery. The judge had all the genius and defects of Swift. In the midst of sober and erudite phrases there would flame forth wild outbursts of scathing wit clothed in fantastic and morbid garb. He introduced from the Bench stories of a humour too broad for the smoking-room. He was the most brilliant of raconteurs, with an inexhaustible fund of apt quotation from a repository that was not only wide but deep, but remarks passed out of his mouth before ever they entered his mind and they brought discredit on the court. He could not control himself, and at times was frightened at seeing in print some of his pronouncements that should not have been deemed printable.

26 IFC Ms. Vol. 1194, p. 544.

27 IFC Ms. Vol. 356.

28 ibid.

29 IFC Ms. Vol. 1194, pp. 544–48. Bribery of witnesses in boundary disputes is frequently referred to in folk sources, and may have been the motivating factor behind this practice.

The impression the sources convey of Judge Adams is that he was very much a 'man of the people' – having a strong sympathy with, and interest in, the concerns of the lower classes. For instance, he is reported as being reluctant to try cases involving politics or land agitation; by steering clear of such matters, he avoided the necessity of making judgments which could prove very unpopular with the local peasantry.[30] On one occasion he was involved in a political case, but managed to come out of it with his reputation preserved. The speakers at a Land League meeting were arrested, along with three girls. They were duly charged (with what offence is not clear), and on the day of the trial, a huge crowd gathered around Newcastle courthouse. The police presence was not sufficient to keep them out, and there were fears of a crush. But Judge Adams, 'a great favourite with the people', appealed successfully for people to disperse quietly.[31] On other, less controversial topics relating to land he was not afraid to let his opinions be known: it is said that he greatly disliked barbed wire, and frequently spoke out against its use, citing injuries caused to cattle by it.[32] Finally, it was said that 'He was a great man for drinking'.[33] A story is told of a case against a widow publican in Cappamore. The hearing was adjourned over the week-end to enable the widow to attend court. On the Saturday night, Adams and his driver went out to the pub:

After drinking *lán a' mhála* on the way out they reached the widow's house and demanded admittance.
'Get away, youx spalpeens. Don't you know that I am up before that bald-headed squinty-eyed little raispín of an Adams in the morning.'[34]

One can assume it did not go too well with this particular publican on her appearance in Adams's court; although, as a rule, Adams had a reputation for being lenient towards publicans and drinkers alike.

30 IFC Ms. Vol. 1193, p. 353.
31 IFC Ms. Vol. 1210, p. 47. It is not clear whether Judge Adams was actually trying the case, or if he was there merely in a personal capacity.
32 ibid., p. 361. On the topic of barbed wire and possible danger to animals, see also *Meara* v. *Daly* (1914) 68 ILT 223.
33 IFC Ms. Vol. 1194, pp. 548, 308.
34 IFC Ms. Vol. 462, p. 349.

Another laudable quality of Judge Adams from the country people's point of view was that he was entertaining. One account tells us that 'Whenever a funny character appeared in court, Judge Adams used to draw them out.'[35] On one occasion, a man corrected the clerk as to the precise time; thereafter, Adams would always ask that same man for the time. Witnesses with particular talents or skills might be asked to display them for the amusement of the court – one was invited to give a demonstration of juggling with caps belonging to onlookers; another named O'Donnell was asked to sing. Having given of his best, he was duly applauded by all, and we are told his case was dismissed (presumably by way of reward).[36]

The unusual levity of atmosphere in Judge Adams's court seems to have attracted eccentrics. We are told that

Judge Adams often tolerated the presence of individuals that other men in his position would not permit. For example, law proceedings in Rathkeale were invariably favoured by the attendance of two individuals of doubtful sanity. But the judge, ever welcoming anybody or anything that would relieve the monotony of legal procedure, always tacitly acquiesced in their coming to court.[37]

One of these individuals would ask Adams's permission to keep his hat on in court, in order to protect his brains from contamination; the other would request permission to bare his head, in order that the circulation of air might assist his mental processes. Judge Adams would always allow both requests, and this game became so common that the crier would often announce the judge's permission before the two individuals had time to make their applications. It was said that one of the men was harmless, but the other had frequent violent outbursts, which culminated in his murdering his wife, before being committed to an asylum, where he died.[38]

---

35 IFC Ms. Vol. 1210, p. 48.
36 IFC Ms. Vol. 1210, p. 48; Vol. 1194, p. 544.
37 IFC Ms. Vol. 1193, p. 358.
38 ibid.; see also IFC Ms. Vol. 1210, p. 48, and A.M. Sullivan, *The last serjeant*, pp. 51–52.

Adams was renowned for his own personal wit and sense of humour; it was said that people would go to court just to hear his comments and witty conversations with witnesses.[39] He appears to have especially enjoyed bamboozling witnesses with wordplay. On one occasion, a plaintiff named Sam Shire won his case. The judge said to him, 'You are a Palatine', to which Sam answered that he was. The judge continued, 'Your father and grandfather also called Samuel?' Again, the answer was affirmative. The judge declared, 'Well then, I hereby declare that you have every right to be styled "Samuel the Third, King of the Palatines"'.[40]

On another occasion, Judge Adams appears to have exceeded the bounds of popular taste. A witness in an assault case was describing the circumstances in which the fight had taken place. When asked who came into the yard, the witness answered, 'Rice and his wife and her daughter.' The judge seized on this, asking if the witness was insinuating that Rice was not the father of his wife's child: 'Everybody in the court knew well that he thought no such a thing and they considered the statement to be most unjust.'[41]

A Tipperary source said that 'Judge Adams was very fond of a joke', and told the following story of a Limerick case involving a fight between harvest-workers.

Judge Adams heard the case with great patience as usual.

> Judge: Is it usual to give refreshments in the harvestry field?
> Farmer: Yes, my Lord, we had the usual quarter cask.
> Judge: And had you a table and chair in the fields?
> Farmer: No, my Lord, no article of furniture is ever taken to the field except a bucket and a few glasses or tumblers.
> Judge: In that case, some of these men were perjuring themselves. They swore that the blow was given with a side-board
> Farmer: That's quite correct. I saw the blow being struck ...

[The Judge enjoyed the situation immediately when he learned that the Tipp[erary] and Limerick pronunciation of 'scythe' is 'sigh' but 'scythe-board' becomes 'side-board'.][42]

39 IFC Ms. Vol. 1194, p. 548.
40 IFC Ms. Vol. 1193, pp. 352–53.
41 IFC Ms. Vol. 1193, p. 351.
42 IFC Ms. Vol. 462, pp. 347–49.

The judge's taste for conversation and banter with witnesses, while entertaining for the masses, could be frustrating for lawyers. Two of our sources mention a case in which a priest was called upon to give evidence. The judge and the priest 'wasted a full half hour talking about the different varieties of snuff to the great disgust of the lawyers.'[43] Of course, it is possible that the lawyers' impatience and frustration served to increase the pleasure of the onlookers, and their liking for this maverick justice.

LAWYERS

Since the time when the interpretation of law and the settlement of disputes became the province of a specialist class, lawyers have seldom enjoyed a good press. Unflattering descriptions of lawyers can claim biblical and classical antecedents: Christ and Cicero both railed against lawyers who, by their sophistry, perverted the purity of the law; twisting its words to serve their own ends. These diatribes form part of a clerical and literary anti-lawyer tradition in Western culture which has been 'matched, if not exceeded by a parallel stream of popular hostility.'[44]

In *The sociology of law*, Cotterrell laid most of the blame for this at the door of law itself:

To many people law seems separate from other aspects of life. It appears as an arcane world of knowledge which is intimidating to the uninitiated in its bulk and obscurity.... Few people other than lawyers discover the mysteries contained in the thousands of volumes of law reports and legal treatises. Legal experience is thought to exist in a different realm from social experience.[45]

Not only is there separation in terms of knowledge and training; but lawyers are also encouraged to cultivate an emotional distance from their clients, in order that their feelings as to what is right and just will not cloud their analysis of the law. This heightens the

---

43 IFC Ms. Vol. 1193, p. 352; Vol. 1194, p. 308. The latter version says that Dublin theatre was also discussed.
44 Prest, *The rise of the barristers*, p. 284.
45 Cotterrell, *Sociology of law*, p. 16.

sense, for both lawyers and lay people, that the legal profession is an exclusive caste. From there, it is but a step to a popular suspicion that lawyers have their own interests and agendas at heart – interests which may be inimical to those of their clients.

Such a suspicion may be reflected in the practice (seemingly widespread in the nineteenth century) of writing wills which provided for the disinheritance of beneficiaries should they seek to challenge the will in court. An example from 1834 is the will of one James Murphy, referred to in Brian Walker's *Sentry Hill: an Ulster farm and family*, which includes the following stipulation:

... if any of My Children should be Dissatisfied with this My Will and put the rest to any trouble they shall forfeit their claim by so doing.[46]

An even more direct statement was found in a will which formed the subject of litigation in the case of *Massy* v. *Rogers*[47]. The testator had ended his disposition of property with the following declaration:

I have now stated my will, to the best of my ability, clearly as to the disposal of my different properties; yet, in order to prevent disputes, I shall add this clause: And it is my will that all differences of opinion as to my intention shall be left to the decision of the executors, whose decision shall be final if they agree; and if they do not, they shall appoint an umpire, from whose judgment there shall be no appeal. Anyone resorting to law, I here cancel and annul every benefit they would otherwise have derived from this my will, and whatever they have forfeited shall be divided by the executors among those who had acceded to their decision. I declare this my last will and testament, this 27th day of March, 1876 ...

Ironically, this very attempt to remove the will from the purview of the law, itself became the subject of a legal challenge. The general principle that parties cannot by contract oust the ordinary courts of their jurisdiction was applied by the court to this situation, and the above clause was held unlawful and inoperative.

46 Brian M. Walker, *Sentry Hill: an Ulster farm and family* (Belfast, 1981), p. 17.
47 (1883) 11 LR Ir 489.

General remarks

Our sources are brimming with sayings and stories which display a sense of the separateness of the legal profession. Thomas Lynch, a Meath farmer, said that lawyers were held in 'a kind of dread' by the people.[48] A popular saying was that lawyers were the real winners in any dispute: 'The law is crooked. You can never tell how a case will go.... The lawyers will be the winners ... no matter how much lawyers fight and squabble over a case they're as great as pickpockets when it's over';[49] 'People have no good opinion at all of lawyers ... whoever wins a law-suit the lawyer always wins';[50] 'Is é an t-ainm ceart Gaeilge ar an "Attorney" an robadóir [robálaí].'[51] A Cavan justice named Waters was praised in one story for suggesting to the parties involved in a particular case that if they didn't drop the action, their lawyers would get everything.[52] The expense of lawyers' fees, combined with a perceived propensity to prolong actions in order to extract maximum financial benefit from them, could also explain the following remarks: 'The old people avoided lawyers if there was any chance of winning a case without them';[53] 'In trespass cases, there wouldn't be a word about a solicitor. They'd say that lawyers should be avoided as much as possible.'[54] Expense was also given as a reason for people drawing their own wills: 'The people didn't object to employing a lawyer for doing it, but they wouldn't employ him when they could get it done for nothing.'[55]

Touring Ireland in 1818, the English MP J.C. Curwen (1756–1828) noted a remark applied to attorneys, 'that a single one starves, but that two make fortunes.'[56] He continued:

I have heard an anecdote of two farmers, who on having some trifling dispute, by accident resorted to the same lawyer. After hearing the

48 IFC Ms. Vol. 1197, p. 124.
49 IFC Ms. Vol. 1195, p. 399.
50 IFC Ms. Vol. 1194, p. 567.
51 'the correct name for an attorney is a robber'. IFC Ms. Vol. 143, p. 2029.
52 IFC Ms. Vol. 1196, p. 61.
53 IFC Ms. Vol. 1196, p. 6.
54 IFC Ms. Vol. 1196, p. 221.
55 IFC Ms. Vol. 1196, p. 401.
56 Curwen, *Observations on the state of Ireland*, i, 355.

whole story from the second client, he lamented it was not in his power to be of use to him, but that he would give him a note to a friend of his hard by, a most able and honorable man, to whom the party might safely trust his cause. As the note could appertain to no one but himself, he made free with the seal, and after reading 'Two geese from the country that have quarrelled, good brother: I'll pluck the one and have sent you the other', he thought it most prudent to exhibit the note, and make offer of a conciliatory shake of the hand, which was wisely accepted by his neighbour.[57]

This is a version of the popular 'plucking the geese' tale, which neatly encapsulates the belief that a lawyer's first loyalty was to his wallet; then to his brothers in the profession; and only then to his unfortunate clients.[58] Note also that the two 'geese' are referred to as being 'from the country' – the town / country divide furthering the impression of the lawyers inhabiting a different cultural world.

Other proverbs and stories deal with the moral character of lawyers in a more vituperative manner: 'Three hours sleep would be enough for a lawyer ... a man would say he'd do a job "by degrees [i.e. decrees], the way lawyers get to heaven" ';[59] 'The warmest corner in hell was the final destination of a lawyer. ... No lawyer would ever see God in his glory.'[60] One is reminded of the porter 'welcoming' equivocators to hell in Shakespeare's *Macbeth* (act 2, scene 3):

Knock, knock. Who's there, in th'other devil's name? Faith, here's an equivocator that could swear in both the scales against either scale, who committed treason enough for God's sake, yet could not equivocate to heaven.

From Cavan comes a poetic epitaph for a deceased lawyer; in one version, extemporised by a young boy as the coffin went past, and in another, read out at an informal gathering of legal colleagues on the eve of the funeral service:

---

57 ibid., pp. 355–56.
58 See *Ulster Folklife*, xiii (1967), 9, 12; also IFC Ms. Vol. 1197, pp. 37, 153, 230; Vol. 1196, p. 185; and see above, p. 9, and below, appendix 3.
59 IFC Ms. Vol. 1195, p. 430.
60 IFC Ms. Vol. 1197, p. 7.

The weather is bad, and that's no wonder
A rogue on top, and four more under[61]
The body is now dead, the soul's on its journey
The devil went to law and sent for an attorney.[62]

The view of lawyers as rogues also emerges from the following anecdote, attributed to Daniel O'Connell:

When O'Connell was Lord Mayor of Dublin, on the first day's sitting his weekly court was, of course, extremely crowded. The tipstaffs tried to clear it. 'Let all persons leave the court that haven't business,' shouted one of these functionaries. 'In Cork,' said O'Connell, 'I remember the crier trying to disperse the crowd by exclaiming, 'All ye blackguards that isn't lawyers, quit the court!'[63]

So much for the opinions expressed through folklore about lawyers as a body. But do they really represent the true feelings of the people towards those lawyers they knew, or were our sources simply repeating the received wisdom of centuries?[64] Do they reflect a time when, for whatever reason, lawyers were held in particular disdain by Irish country people? Or are they simply a repetition of age-old social stereotypes, which in reality were not taken seriously by the majority of people? How can these sayings and stories be reconciled with the popular enthusiasm for litigation which outside observers and historians record? Once again, caution should be our watchword when seeking to draw definite conclusions from oral sources.

It is clear, for instance, that traditional antipathy towards lawyers did not stop the people of Mayo from availing of their services at petty sessions, from the 1820s onwards. MacCabe writes that 'By the mid-1830s at least twelve attornies [solicitors] plied the Mayo petty sessions circuit, hired apparently by almost everyone, for almost every kind of case'.[65] The undoubted advantages of having

---

61 A reference to the corpse in the coffin, being carried by four more lawyers.
62 IFC Ms. Vol. 1195, p. 431; see also Vol. 1197, p. 7.
63 *ILT & SJ*, xxxi (1897), 364.
64 See also Prest, *The rise of the barristers*, pp. 285–87.
65 MacCabe, 'Magistrates, peasants, and the petty sessions courts: Mayo 1823–50', *Cathair na Mart*, v (1985), 45, 50.

legal representation should not be forgotten either: in addition to their legal knowledge and skill in cross-examination, the use of a lawyer changed the relationship between the ordinary litigant and the magistrate. Having legal representation gave the litigant a formal dignity which he would not have possessed in the kind of informal, 'private chamber' hearings which preceded the rise of petty sessions. With a good and clever lawyer, even the poorest farmer or labourer could strike at targets above their station, with some hope of success.

Good and clever lawyers

While country people do not have a good word to say about lawyers in general, some individuals are praised – among them, Daniel O'Connell, Isaac Butt, Risteard Ó Mathúna, and John Philpott Curran.[66] In the main, they are feted for their ability to use cleverness and trickery to secure victory for their clients. But before looking at some of these stories, it is important to place them in the context of the age which spawned them.

It would seem that, in Ireland at least, the common law system in the eighteenth and nineteenth centuries was characterised by an exaltation of the letter of the law, often at the expense of its spirit. Procedural rules, detailed statutes and complex precedents proliferated. McDowell, in *Ireland in the age of imperialism and revolution, 1760–1801*, talks of an 'emphasis on a meticulous observance of procedural rules'.[67] Similar studies have not been made for the nineteenth century, but the popular perception of how lawyers won cases is, to my mind, strong evidence that such an attitude persisted. A large volume of folk narratives involving court cases end with victory being secured by some form of technical or clever wordplay, often verging on the ludicrous.

Take for instance a Tipperary tale of a classical tutor who abducted the young daughter of a rich Protestant lawyer. When caught, the tutor managed to escape conviction by arguing that,

---

66 On the topic of 'good lawyers' in popular opinion, see also Prest, op. cit., pp. 312–22.
67 McDowell, *Ireland in the age of imperialism and revolution, 1760–1801* (Oxford, 1979), pp. 543–44.

as the girl had been placed in front of him on the saddle of his horse, she was technically abducting him! In a twist which would no doubt have given extra pleasure to the storyteller's audience, the idea for such a defence had come originally from the girl's father, before he realised who it was had been abducted.[68] This tale can clearly be placed in the land of fantasy. Its significance lies not in its veracity, but in the fact that such a tale would be told at all: it stems from an underlying popular assumption that the law sometimes did produce absurd results.

A tale from Kerry sounds equally far-fetched, but is in fact within the bounds of possibility: it concerns a man named Ó Raogáin who was called up for jury service. Before going, he filled his pockets with food. The jury heard a case of sheep-stealing, and at the end of it, all were agreed on a guilty verdict except Ó Raogáin. A unanimous verdict being required, the jury were forced to remain in their room, arguing the issues. At length, after two days and nights without food, the other jurors caved in; Ó Raogáin got his way, and the accused was freed.[69] Incredible as it may seem, this could have happened; for it was not until the Juries Procedure (Ireland) Act 1876 that juries in Ireland were allowed, at the trial judge's discretion, to receive 'reasonable refreshment' at any time before the giving of their verdict.[70]

Large numbers of stories are told of Daniel O'Connell; again, most are implausible. In one, O'Connell tells a convicted criminal to knock off the judge's black cap as he is about to pronounce the death sentence. This done, O'Connell proclaims the sentence to be invalid, and the prisoner is freed.[71] At the beginning of another case, the judge asks O'Connell to 'do all you can for the prisoner'. O'Connell thereupon brings the prisoner into another room and allows him to escape. The judge is confounded by his own words, and can do nothing.[72] A Cavan tale has O'Connell persuading a landlord about to evict a priest to sign a contract allowing the

68 IFC Ms. Vol. 517, p. 430.
69 IFC Ms. Vol. 1004, p. 306.
70 Juries Procedure (Ireland) Act, 1876, s.12.
71 Uí Ogáin, *Immortal Dan*, p. 127.
72 ibid., p. 135.

clergyman to stay 'from today till tomorrow' – since tomorrow never comes, the landlord finds he can never legally carry out the eviction.[73]

Another folk narrative tells of an occasion when Isaac Butt defended a man accused of murder. It was written in the charge that the victim 'died of the bullet' which the accused was alleged to have fired. Butt was able to secure an acquittal by demonstrating that death was actually caused, not by the bullet, but by the extraction of the bullet in the hospital.[74] This is a version of a true story. A man named Talbot, who had acted as a government spy from within the Fenian movement, was shot at point-blank range one night in Dublin. Talbot was brought to the Richmond Hospital, where he underwent two successive operations in order to have the bullet removed. As it turned out, no bullet was found by the doctor in charge of the operations. Talbot died one week later. Butt defended the man who had fired the shot, a man named Kelly. He succeeded in convincing the jury that the victim died, not from the bullet wound, but from a brain haemorrhage caused by the incompetence of the doctor conducting the operations. Kelly was found not guilty of murder. Because of its political overtones, the case gained a considerable notoriety, and helped elevate Butt into a figure of national importance. Kelly was acquitted, re-arrested and charged with shooting at the policemen who had captured him. He was convicted and sentenced to twenty years penal servitude. But this would only have served to increase Isaac Butt's reputation amongst ordinary people, as further evidence that by verbal trickery he had managed to persuade a jury of a guilty man's innocence.[75]

A Mayo tale tells of how Sir Niall Ó Domhnaill sent his son away to become a lawyer, and to learn *an ceart agus an mícheart* – right and wrong. After seven years, the son returned to announce that he had learned 'right'; his father promptly sent him back again to learn 'wrong'. When he returned again, the son went to

---

73 IFC Ms. Vol. 1197, p. 179.
74 IFC Ms. Vol. 1196, p. 61.
75 For a fuller account of the Talbot case see Terence de Vere White, *The road of excess* (Dublin, 1946), pp. 253–58.

his father's steward, getting him to kill one of Sir Niall's pigs. The steward and the son divided the carcass equally between them. In due course, Sir Niall prosecuted the steward for theft, and Sir Niall's son was engaged for the defence. The son declared in court that the steward 'had no more of the pig than I had', and his declaration resulted in the steward's acquittal – an underhand victory which showed that the son had learned 'wrong' as well as 'right'.[76]

A similar ruse was used by O'Connell when appearing as a character witness for a man charged with some unrecorded crime. Before the trial, O'Connell sold the man a pair of shoes for eight pence. When asked in court how long he had known the accused, O'Connell replied, 'From the time when his shoes cost only four pence [each].' On the strength of O'Connell's impressive testimony to his character, the accused man was freed.[77] Both this case and the Ó Domhnaill case are interesting in that they rely not only on clever wordplay, but also upon the reputation of the witness as an honest, upright member of society. O'Connell and the son of Niall Ó Domhnaill do not lie outright; but they succeed by not revealing the whole truth. Exaggerated though these stories may be, to me they display an instinctive grasp of the subtlety of an advocate's job – being not to create or condone untruth, but rather to choose which parts of the truth to emphasise in the courtroom.

Verbal trickery also occurs in a tale of a disputed will – an archetypal folk story. The story appears in two forms, but the same trick is at work in both. The validity of a deceased's signature on a purported will is challenged. The beneficiaries all appear in court and swear that 'life was in him' when the will was made. It turns out that what they mean by this is that a fly was placed in the man's mouth after his death, while his hand was used to write a bogus will. In one version of the story, the lawyer for the other side (usually O'Connell) forces them to admit the ruse in court; in the other version, it is the lawyer who puts them up to it, and the plan succeeds.[78]

76 IFC Ms. Vol. 794, p. 491. See also Uí Ógáin, *Immortal Dan*, p. 125.
77 Uí Ógáin, *Immortal Dan*, p. 126.
78 IFC Ms. Vol. 693, pp. 16–17; Vol. 1458, p. 360. See also Uí Ogáin, *Immortal*

Lawyers and witnesses

As we shall see in a later chapter,[79] the wit, imagination, loyalty to friend or kin, and unwillingness to be constrained by the truth of Irish witnesses could make them formidable courtroom opponents. In the circumstances, it is not surprising that outside observers were often especially impressed with the abilities of Irish barristers and attorneys (solicitors) in cross-examination. Henry Inglis wrote: 'I was much struck at Ennis, as I had been at Tralee, with the acuteness and talent of the Irish attorneys. Their cross-examinations of witnesses were admirable; certainly not surpassed by the very best cross-examinations I ever heard from the mouth of an English barrister.'[80] In Baileboro, Co. Cavan, a much-liked and admired attorney was one Frank McBreen. A folk source singled out from his many virtues, his ability to handle opposing witnesses: 'He was a good, sound man with good ideas and he was very sympathetic. But when it was called for, he was severe in cross-examining witnesses.'[81] In this section we shall look at some of the ways in which lawyers were said to overcome witnesses for other parties. Stories which see witnesses triumph over lawyers are reserved for another chapter.[82]

In assailing the testimony of opposing witnesses, two principal techniques were used: one was to attack the person's character; the other was to trip them up verbally, by forcing them into some confused admission that would detract from their overall credibility.[83] William Curran witnessed, with grudging admiration, the employment of both techniques by Daniel O'Connell at the trial of one Larry Cronan. Larry was charged with offences which would have seen him hung if convicted, and there were a number of witnesses willing to attest to his guilt. Luckily for him, the Counsellor was at hand: 'From some of the witnesses he extracted that they were unworthy of all credit, being notorious knaves, or

---

Dan, p. 134; Thompson, *Motif-index,* J 1140 (cleverness in detection of the truth), K 362.7 (signature forged to obtain money).
79 Below, chapter 5.
80 Inglis, *Ireland in 1834,* p. 293.
81 IFC Ms. Vol. 1195, p. 425.
82 Below, chapter 5.
83 See McDowell, *Ireland in the age of imperialism,* p. 544.

process-servers. Others he inveigled into a metaphysical puzzle touching the prisoner's identity....'[84]

In the folklore archives, many of the tricks attributed to O'Connell are improper, verging on unethical. In many cases, they succeed in freeing a man whom everyone knew to be guilty. The popularity of these stories clearly implies a gulf between law and justice in the folk mind, and a belief that lawyers placed far more importance on winning cases than on the truth. One common archetype has O'Connell defending a man accused of murder, whose hat was found at the scene of the crime. While cross-examining a witness to the murder, O'Connell holds the hat up, and invites the witness to swear that this was the hat he saw at the scene of the crime. This done, O'Connell then pretends to read from a label inside the hat bearing the accused's name or initials. Anxious to bolster his testimony, the witness swears that the label was on the hat found at the scene. The Counsellor then shows the court that no such label in fact exists, and the otherwise trust-worthy evidence of the witness is completely discredited. In most versions of the story, the accused man is actually guilty of the murder, but escapes justice thanks to O'Connell's cleverness.[85]

Time and again in folk narratives, lawyers win cases by estab-lishing confusion in the mind of a witness over small details. O'Connell was once said to have defended a man who had stolen a number of shirts. In court, the Counsellor wore a shirt of precisely the same description as those stolen; the victim of the theft (who was the principal witness) was then induced to claim that this shirt was indeed one of those stolen from him. O'Connell refuted this allegation by proving he had purchased it elsewhere, and used this unfortunate outburst to fatally discredit the theft-victim's testimony.[86] A tale told in Galway and Mayo has an attorney successfully defend a man who stole a horse, by claiming that the horse in fact belonged to the attorney. This lie is supported by the trick of nailing shoes with the attorney's name and address on the

---

84 Curran, *Sketches of the Irish bar* (London, 1855), p. 287.
85 IFC Ms. Vol. 1147, p. 576; Vol. 1196, p. 63. See also Uí Ógáin, *Immortal Dan*, pp. 133–34.
86 Uí Ógáin, *Immortal Dan*, p. 127.

horse. In the Mayo version, the attorney is not actually acting for the accused, but enters the court as a witness.[87]

These stories are similar to an international folk motif, noted by Aarne-Thompson,[88] in which a trickster, summoned to court on the complaint of a Jew refuses to go unless he has a new coat. The Jew lends him his. In court, the trickster accuses the Jew of being a liar, saying: 'He will even claim that I am wearing his coat.' The Jew does so, but no-one believes him. His testimony is discredited.

In a Donegal tale, a poor lawyer robbed a landlord's agent. A gentleman's son was wrongly convicted of the crime, and he asked the lawyer to conduct his appeal. In court, the lawyer put on a cap which had been found at the scene of the crime. The key witness then recognised him, and declared him to be the real thief. The lawyer denied this apparently preposterous accusation, and the witness's testimony was effectively destroyed. It is said that the lawyer was never poor again.[89]

From Kerry comes a tale of a barrister named Risteard Ó Mathúna, who appears to have gained himself a considerable reputation in his local area: 'Chuala go m'bfhearr é ná an Consailéar [i.e. Daniel O'Connell] chun duine a thabhairt saor ón ndlí.'[90] In this particular tale, Ó Mathúna was acting for a woman who was accused of stealing a goose from a neighbour who owed her money. The principal witness was a boy who saw her returning from the neighbour's house at night with a goose. In cross-examination, Ó Mathúna asked the boy whether it was a goose or a gander that he saw. The boy was unable to say with certainty what sex the animal was, but as he had already sworn that it was a goose, his evidence was deemed unreliable, and the woman escaped judgment. A similar line of attack was used by O'Connell when defending two men accused of murdering an Orangeman (in retaliation for an earlier murder of a Catholic): he

87 IFC Ms. Vol. 488, p. 341; Vol. 258, p. 312.
88 Thompson, *Motif-index*, J 1151.2.
89 IFC Ms. Vol. 444, p. 420. A version of the tale from Kerry is at IFC Ms. Vol. 984, p. 27.
90 'I heard he was better than the Counsellor [i.e. Daniel O'Connell] at freeing a person from the law.' IFC Ms. Vol. 1006, p. 78.

was able to pinpoint confusion in the mind of the relevant witness as to whether the weapon used was a stick or an iron bar, and the case was dismissed.[91]

One final archetype involves attacking the impartiality of a witness, by a ruse which is as symmetrically pleasing as it is professionally unethical. Before the case comes up for hearing, the defence lawyer approaches the key prosecution witness informally, and places a bet with him on the outcome of the case. In court, counsel reveals the existence of this bet, and successfully impugns the reliability of the prosecution witness on that ground – using the bet to win the case, and thereby winning the bet also.[92]

PROCESS-SERVERS

In William Curran's account of the trial of Larry Cronan (referred to earlier), he talks of O'Connell proving the unreliability of witnesses by showing them to be 'notorious knaves or process servers'[93] – an eloquent testimony to the low esteem in which process-servers were held. This is hardly surprising; a profession which consisted of delivering bad news to unwilling and occasionally violent recipients was never likely to attract the cream of the labour market. In Baileboro, a story is told of how, one day, a process-server named Kent arrived into court, drunk. The judge turned to his clerk in exasperation and exclaimed, 'Why don't you get some decent man for this job!' Kent roused himself and replied, 'To tell you the truth, my Lord, no decent man would take the job.'[94] This particular process-server's problems went beyond mere job satisfaction; according to another folklore source, 'He cut his throat in the finish.'[95]

The inherent perils of the profession are reflected in the demeanour of Dan Hogan, a process-server in *The collegians*: 'You may read something of his vocation in the side-long glance of his

---

91 IFC Ms. Vol. 1196, p. 118.
92 IFC Ms. Vol. 1269, p. 453. See also Uí Ogáin, *Immortal Dan*, pp. 122–24.
93 See above, pp. 79–80.
94 IFC Ms. Vol. 1195, p. 470.
95 IFC Ms. Vol. 1195, p. 438.

eye, and in the paltry deprecating air of his whole demeanour. He starts, as if afraid of a blow, whenever anyone addresses him.'[96]

Not everyone hated process-servers, but it can safely be said that nobody liked them.[97] Tolerant disdain is about the most positive attitude evinced by the folklore sources towards these unfortunates: 'there wasn't much ill-feeling against [them], but nobody cared to see them coming about the house';[98] 'Process-servers weren't popular';[99] 'The people would "bid them the time of day" but not a lot more, and in a lot of cases they wouldn't.'[100] Others were not so tolerant: 'The informer and process-server were nearly on a level, but the informer was the worst of all.'[101]

One Cavan informant said he never heard of a process-server being beaten.[102] A man from Meath said that people were generally afraid to molest them,[103] but a number of tales indicate the contrary. A popular, though probably apocryphal story, found in Cavan, Donegal, Galway, Cork and Kerry, tells of a process-server being forced to eat the documents he was supposed to deliver.[104] A Monaghan source told folklore collectors that process-servers would get 'an odd beating', and that they kept clear of the town on fair days and holidays.[105] A colleague of the aforementioned Kent, named Gillis, used to carry a stick when on duty; which makes one wonder whether it was for protection. A Limerick source talked of a process-server who was attacked, stripped and beaten by Moonlighters while on his way home one night.[106] A man from Cavan said that process-servers often had boiling water or stones thrown at them by women, when they came to a house.[107]

96 Griffin, *The collegians*, p. 96.
97 IFC Ms. Vol. 1833, p. 251.
98 IFC Ms. Vol. 1195, p. 490.
99 IFC Ms. Vol. 1196, p. 252.
100 IFC Ms. Vol. 1196, p. 7.
101 IFC Ms. Vol. 1196, p. 25.
102 IFC Ms. Vol. 1196, p. 369.
103 IFC Ms. Vol. 1196, p. 282.
104 IFC Ms. Vol. 1197, pp. 174, 216, 269; Vol. 43, p. 66; Vol. 171, p. 276; Vol. 271, pp. 372–75; Vol. 962, pp. 125–30; Vol. 850, pp. 581–82; Vol. 929, p. 379; Vol. 1195, p. 439; Vol. 1196, p. 314.
105 IFC Ms. Vol. 1096, p. 301.
106 IFC Ms. Vol. 1194, p. 570.
107 IFC Ms. Vol. 1197, p. 47.

In the French peasant village of Zola's *La terre*, a bailiff who doubled as a process-server suffered similar indignities:

Vimeux was a very grubby little shrimp of a man with a tiny yellow tuft of beard from which emerged a red nose and a pair of rheumy eyes. Always dressed like a gentleman, in a hat, a frock-coat and black trousers, dreadfully worn and stained, he was celebrated in the region for the frightful drubbings he had received at the hands of the peasants when delivering notice of proceedings against them, in remote areas where he was defenceless. There were many legends about him, thrashings and involuntary duckings in ponds, a mile-long chase at the point of a pitchfork, a sound spanking administered, with his trousers down, by a mother and her daughter.[108]

Later on in the novel, Vimeux is further humiliated by having a chamber-pot emptied on his head from the attic window of a house where he had come to serve a summons.

Finally, returning to Ireland, we find some stories of process-servers who were killed. A Mayo account tells of a process-server named Huddy who was murdered by being drowned in Lough Mask.[109] In Waterford county, apparently, a professional assassin named Cathal Ruadh killed a process-server who had served a relative of his with an eviction notice.[110] And the following bizarre tale, told to a folk collector in 1931, comes from the village of Doon in Co. Tipperary:

A young man named Woods ... came to Father Patrick ... P.P. of Doon about 40 years ago and expressed a wish to become Catholic. As he was under 18 years in age the Protestant Church Body took legal proceedings against the P.P. The process-server found it absolutely impossible to serve the necessary document on him.

Finally he arrived in Doon when the priest was hearing [confessions] and entered the box as if he were going to Confession. As soon as the priest pulled back the slide, he served the writ and left the box. Father Patrick came out immediately with the blue document in his hand ... The women of Doon stoned the unfortunate process-server to death.[111]

---

108   Emile Zola, *La terre (the earth)* (Harmondsworth, 1980), p. 323. *La terre* was first published in 1887.
109   IFC Ms. Vol. 1196, p. 191.
110   IFC Ms. Vol. 84, pp. 374–75.
111   IFC Ms. Vol. 407, pp. 203–04; and see below, p. 146.

BAILIFFS, GRIPPERS

If the process-server was a bearer of bad news, how much more so were the bailiffs and 'grippers', whose job involved the seizure of goods for non-payment of rent (a legal remedy, feudal in origin, known as distress),[112] and the carrying out of eviction orders. One folklore source said that 'Any liking they had for a bailiff he forced it on them.... Grippers and bailiffs were a class of people that weren't respected and neither were the process-servers.' The same speaker recalled a gripper known as 'Bull' Smith: 'He got more battering with sticks than would kill several men. They'd beat him in public houses and every place they could get at him.'[113] Another man said of grippers in general that 'They'd get beatings. You'd get one man to be afraid of them, and you'd get other men that wouldn't.'[114]

A Cavan man remembered seeing a gripper named Smith being stoned while seizing cattle.[115] In Galway, a bailiff took the only cow of an old man in lieu of unpaid rent; three or four local lads set upon him as he walked up the road, and recaptured the cow. Some local women helped them to escape.[116] An Antrim source recalled a bailiff named McAuley being attacked while serving processes, and forced to tear each process in half with his teeth, in order to give people more time to pay overdue rent.[117]

During his stay on the Aran Islands, John Millington Synge wrote a fascinating piece in his diary concerning attempts to levy distress on islanders who had been defaulting in their debts:

112 For a history of the remedy of distress see Alan Dowling, 'A parliamentary history of the law of distress for rent from 1845', in N. Dawson, D. Greer and P. Ingram (ed.), *One hundred and fifty years of Irish law* (Belfast, 1996), p. 171.
113 IFC Ms. Vol. 1195, pp. 378, 470.
114 IFC Ms. Vol. 1195, p. 477.
115 IFC Ms. Vol. 1196, p. 186. See also *Kinsella* v. *Hamilton* (1890) 26 LR Ir 671.
116 IFC Ms. Vol. 433, pp. 351–53.
117 IFC Ms. Vol. 1360, p. 155; Vol. 43, p. 66.

Till this year no-one on the island would consent to act as bailiff, so that it was impossible to identify the cattle of the defaulters. Now, however, a man of the name of Patrick has sold his honour, and the effort of concealment is practically futile. This falling away from the ancient loyalty of the island has caused intense indignation....[118]

As events unfolded, Synge was to realise that 'indignation' was wholly inadequate to describe the depth of emotion felt by the islanders at this betrayal. Early warning was given in the form of a threatening note left on the doorpost of the chapel, saying, 'Patrick, the devil, a revolver is waiting for you ...'. On the day that Patrick commenced his duties on the island, the entire population came out to jeer and abuse him. There, in front of her friends and neighbours, Patrick's mother solemnly cursed him aloud. Synge was deeply moved: 'On these islands the women live only for their children, and it is hard to estimate the power of the impulse that made this old woman stand out and curse her son.'[119]

On that occasion, despite the depth of feeling and resentment, the crowd did not physically attack Patrick. Perhaps they were inhibited by the thought of the power which he now wielded, and the ways in which he might retaliate. A Cavan source said that 'The bailiff could serve an ejectment notice on you if you didn't take off your hat to him when you met him in the road, and I knew of him to do it.'[120] He added that he had heard some stories of bailiffs being attacked, but not many: '... generally the people were too much afraid to do it. If you hit a bailiff in them days you nearly might as well be up for attempted murder.'[121]

A bailiff with a reputation for abuse of power in Co. Clare was Big Jack O'Reilly from Kilgalligan:

Like most bailiffs of his kind he was an oppressor and with sternness he dominated and exercised his despotism over the Community amongst whom he lived.... Many misdeeds could be quoted against him. He even

---

118 Synge, *The Aran islands* (Oxford, 1979), p. 88. *The Aran islands* was first
      published in 1907.
119 ibid.
120 IFC Ms. Vol. 1195, p. 437.
121 ibid.

used to intercept the fishermen on their returning from fishing and compel them [to] hand over to him any quantity of fish which he demanded.[122]

Finally, there are some stories which indicate that not all bailiffs and grippers were hated; for instance, the gripper William McCleary was regarded as 'a decent man', because he would often warn those on whom he was due to call to remove their goods and livestock before he came.[123] Another, named Barney Carroll, was known as a good scholar and 'a legal man'; he wrote nearly all letters from the locals to their friends and relatives in America, and drew up all the wills in the area.[124]

REVENUE MEN, GAUGERS

A detailed study of the role of customs officers, revenue men or 'gaugers', as they were sometimes called, is beyond the scope of this book.[125] Nor is it possible to examine in any detail the culture of illicit distillation in Ireland over the last few hundred years. But in order to understand popular attitudes to 'revenue men' (the revenue police) and gaugers, it is necessary to give a brief summary of their role.

Gaugers and surveyors worked for the Board of Excise. Their duties involved the inspection of licensed distilleries, and the suppression of illegal whiskey-making. To assist them in the seizure of stills and the making of arrests, they would call on the services of the army. The military were never particularly enamoured of this duty, and by 1817 all co-operation between the two bodies had ceased. In 1818, the revenue police were formed: at first, they could only act in conjunction with the gaugers; but from 1823 onwards, the Excise Board gave the police excise commissions which allowed them to take advantage of the gaugers' statutory powers of entry, search and seizure. Despite their efforts, however, illicit distillation was not wiped out. The revenue police were disbanded in 1857.

122 IFC Ms. Vol. 1244, pp. 561–63.
123 IFC Ms. Vol. 1197, p. 42.
124 IFC Ms. Vol.1197, p. 89.
125 Those wishing to read a fuller history of the revenue police and their activities might begin with an article by Norma Dawson, 'Illicit distillation

Considering the ubiquity of illegal distilling in the eighteenth and nineteenth centuries, there is surprisingly little mention of revenue officers in folklore sources. From what there is, we might surmise that gaugers and revenue-men (the terms are largely synonymous in the folk mind) were regarded with mixed feelings. One story tells of a gauger and the devil walking the roads together. As they neared a poteen-house they saw a woman outside it driving ducks. Two ducks escaped from her into the river, and the woman exclaimed, 'May the devil take you anyway.' 'There's a job for you', said the gauger to the devil; but the devil refused, saying that the curse had not come from the woman's heart. The woman then looked up, saw the gauger and cried, 'May the devil take that bailiff [i.e. the gauger]' – the devil duly obliged her.[126] Even more damning is the text of a Sligo song called 'The drowning of the revenue men', supposedly written by one Pat Ryan of Ballindoon in the 1830s. Based on a tragedy that befell 24 revenue men who had attacked poteen-makers on Inishmore, the song is regrettably incomplete; but the closing stanzas convey hatred and contempt to a depth which implies the excise officers must have done more than merely seize illicit whiskey:

But may the scurvey and fever, sweep Laudley the gauger
To regions of torture that are not on the Earth
And may Oscar the great with his flail of great weight
Pursue his companions, and thrash them to death.

So let this be a warning, both noon night, and morning
To all Roman Catholics for evermore
To have nothing to do, with that hellish crew
That went still hunting, into Inishmore.

Now come all you millers, and poteen distillers
Get your utensils, and flourish once more
Since these Brinsley slashers, and infamous smashers
Are food for the fishes, far, far from the shore.[127]

and the revenue police in Ireland in the eighteenth and nineteenth centuries', *Ir Jur*, xii (1977), 282.
126 IFC Ms. Vol. 1195, p. 378.
127 IFC Ms. Vol. 485, p. 154.

In contrast, another story (from the same Cavan source as the story of the devil) portrays a kindly revenue officer. It seems that a publican who purchased poteen regularly from a particular source, tricked the poteen-maker into selling poteen to a revenue officer. The officer told the poteen-maker who he was, but proceeded to fine the publican £500 on the spot. He gave that money to the poteen-maker, on condition that he cease his illegal activities from that moment on.[128]

Folklore sources are generally aware that the revenue-men antedated the peelers;[129] they are also aware of the narrow ambit of their duties. One man said that 'except in certain cases, they wouldn't arrest anyone, for their principal business was the quelling of the poteen-running.'[130] Another said they would not interfere in brawls, fights or the like.[131] One Cavan source said that they would fine anyone they caught in possession of an unlicensed gun; another said that they engaged in no police work other than the suppression of illicit distilling.[132]

A Clare man said that they wouldn't visit isolated areas too often, though whether due to lack of resources or fear of ambush is not stated.[133] Caesar Otway recorded a story in which a revenue officer was ambushed, kidnapped and held for six weeks. He was not neglected during his capture, being 'well fed on trout, grouse, hares and chickens; plenty of poteen mixed with the pure water of the lake was his portion to drink.'[134] It turned out that a law had been passed which 'made the townland on which the still was found, or any part of the process of distillation detected, liable to a heavy fine, to be levied indiscriminately on all landholders.'[135] The revenue officer concerned had amassed evidence which would have resulted in a collective fine of £7,000 being imposed

128 IFC Ms.Vol. 1195, pp. 452–55.
129 For example, IFC Ms.Vol. 1838, p. 228.
130 IFC Ms.Vol. 1196, p. 88.
131 IFC Ms.Vol. 1196, p. 492.
132 IFC Ms.Vol. 1195, p. 497; Vol. 1196, p. 367.
133 IFC Ms.Vol. 38, p. 210.
134 Otway, *Sketches in Ireland* (Dublin, 1827), p. 64.
135 ibid., p. 65.

on the district: accordingly, he was kidnapped and held until the assizes were over, then released. Shortly afterwards, Otway tells us, 'this imprudent and unconstitutional law was repealed'.[136]

136   ibid., p. 67. The first law fining townlands for breaches of the excise laws was passed in 1785 (25 Geo. III, c.34). The system was suspended from 1810 until 1813 (50 Geo. III, c.15; 52 Geo. III, c.97; 53 Geo. III, c.148; 54 Geo. III, c.32) and for a brief period in 1816 (56 Geo. III, c.112, s.21). In 1820 an indefinite suspension of the system was passed (59 Geo. III, c.98). This lasted until its final abolition in 1831 (1 & 2 Will. IV, c.55, s.54).

CHAPTER FIVE

Appearing in court

AS WE HAVE SEEN,[1] attitudes to law in Ireland can be divided into two broad camps: there were those who feared and mistrusted law, seeking to avoid it wherever possible; and there were others (probably a majority) for whom law held no terrors; they embraced it with enthusiasm and relished any opportunity to come before judge or magistrate. Following on from this, one is tempted to assume there were but two types of witnesses – the reluctant and the eager – but that would be a gross oversimplification. Many factors operated to affect the attitudes of those who appeared in court. They include: the disposition and personalities of the witnesses themselves; the circumstances of the case; the existence of kinship or other bonds between the witness and one or more of the parties; the use of bribery and other inducements; the seriousness of the charge or claim being addressed; and the abilities of the lawyers and justices in court. Bearing these and other factors in mind, it is possible nonetheless to identify two principal patterns of behaviour adopted by the Irish countryman when under examination in court – one might term them the 'extrovert' and 'introvert' patterns of witness behaviour.

Extrovert

This style is characterised by an overt willingness to talk and to answer questions, which in fact serves to hide the more vulnerable aspects of one's evidence beneath a welter of rhetoric and skilful wordplay – in effect, employing the techniques of lawyers against them. As in tennis, the trick is to return your opponent's serve with speed and gusto, while adding a certain spin of your own to the ball in the hope of deceiving him. To successfully battle with lawyers and magistrates in this way demanded a degree

---

1 See generally above, chapter 2.

of composure and self-confidence bordering on arrogance: many Irish people seem to have possessed this in abundance. James Johnson, writing in 1844 following a tour of Ireland, made a comparison between John Bull ('Johnny') and his neighbour Paddy in terms of behaviour in the witness box. He wrote that

Johnny has not half the talent, wit or genius for 'bilking the barrister', and defeating law, that his neighbour Pat possesses. The latter never dreams of going into a witness-box, merely as a witness, but as a lawyer, to advocate the cause of his patron, clan or party, and puzzle the opposing counsel and clients.[2]

Carleton describes the typical Irish peasant undergoing cross-examination as having

... a versatility of talent that keeps him always ready; a happiness of retort, generally disastrous to the wit of the most established cross-examiner; an apparent simplicity, which is quite as impenetrable as the lawyer's assurance; a *vis comica*, which puts the court in tears; and an originality of sorrow, that often convulses it with laughter. His resources, when he is pressed, are inexhaustible; and the address with which he contrives to gain time, that he may suit his reply to the object of his evidence, is beyond all praise.[3]

Maurice Healy's humorous depiction of the typical Kerry witness is similar in tone and sentiment, and merits reproduction at length, for reasons both of education and entertainment:

The Englishman goes into a court of law unwillingly, fearfully, and expecially apprehensive of cross-examination. No doubt there are occasional witnesses of that kind in Ireland too; but the vast majority go to give their evidence as a cricketer walks to the wicket. Each is confident he will not be bowled until he has knocked up a good score; each is very disappointed if the bowler limits his efforts to preventing the score from rising, and does not attack his wicket.... The witness would settle himself in the chair with which every Irish witness is accommodated, and

2   Johnson, *A tour in Ireland* (London, 1844), pp. 275–76.
3   Carleton, *Traits and stories*, 2nd series, i, 274.

would turn upon the enemy 'a glance serene and high', which he would renew from time to time during his examination, especially when he thought he had scored a hit. He would answer his own counsel condescendingly, much as the gardener might explain to you about the roses; and every now and then he would turn to the Judge in a friendly way and explain the effect of his last answer so as to make it easy for him. As the opposing advocate stood up to cross-examine him, he would stiffen; every faculty brought under strict control, he would listen to the first question, to see if he could not get in something really contemptuous in his reply. Sometimes he would merely turn to the Judge with a pitying smile, as much as to say: 'Will you listen to what this poor omadhaun is asking me!' At other times his eye would sweep around the galleries, much as Mr Gladstone might have emphasised a point by turning a flashing glance towards his supporters.[4]

Healy goes on to illustrate how the extrovert witness used bluster and blarney to avoid the unpleasant necessity of giving a direct answer to a direct question:

Instead of [an] awkward silence ... there would [be] an indignant repetition of the question, followed by an immediate turn towards the Judge, who would be swamped in a deluge of irrelevant matter, as though it were a complete explanation of the problem under examination; and by the time the witness would be brought back to the point he would have thought of a plausible answer to the actual question he had been asked.[5]

In *The collegians*, Gerald Griffin shows us two masters of the extrovert style. One is Danny, the servant of Hardress Cregan, who murders Eily O'Connor on his master's behalf. When at length he is arrested and charged with the crime, he succeeds in baffling the magistrates despite his outwardly compliant attitude: 'His answers were all given in the true style of Irish witnesses, seeming to evince the utmost frankness, yet invariably leaving the querist in still greater perplexity than before he put the question.'[6]

Following him comes Poll Naughten, a cousin of Danny's, in whose house Eily was kept from the time of her abduction until

4   Healy, *The old Munster circuit*, pp. 90–91.
5   ibid., pp. 91–92.
6   Griffin, *The collegians*, p. 373.

her murder. She too affects a desire to assist the court, but her voluble testimony serves more to confuse than to illuminate, and she consistently evades the one question of importance which is asked of her.[7] Her most dangerous moment comes early on in her evidence, when one of the magistrates asks her directly, 'Did you know the deceased, Eily O'Connor?' Poll replies, 'I never knew a girl o' that name.'[8] This is a blatant lie; but Griffin reminds us that, at the time Poll first met Eily, Eily was newly married to Hardress Cregan. By denying a knowledge of Eily under her *maiden* name, Poll believed she was not in fact committing perjury at all.[9] This is symptomatic of the legalistic attitude to perjury which surfaces in such practices as kissing the thumb rather than the bible (which Poll herself was caught doing), or distinguishing between oaths taken on 'the law bible' from those sworn on a Catholic bible or holy relic.[10] It is also indicative of the kind of wordplay which lawyers were said by the folk to indulge in and encourage, to the inevitable frustration of justice.[11]

A folk story which displays a similar faith in casuistry concerns a dispute over land boundaries. An 'expert' or supposedly independent witness is bribed by one of the parties to fill his shoes with clay from that party's field. Hence, in court, the witness can swear with impunity that wherever he stood, he stood on that party's soil.[12] This story is an internationally recognised archetype, found in Scotland, Denmark, Italy and elsewhere.[13]

Introvert

For those without the talent or inclination to trade blow for blow with counsel and magistrate, an alternative was to say nothing – or as little as possible. Ignorance of law and language was easily feigned, and could form a most effective, if less entertaining, barrier between the court and the truth.

---

7   ibid., pp. 377–79.
8   ibid., p. 377.
9   ibid., p. 380.
10 See below, chapter 6.
11 See above, chapter 4.
12 IFC Ms. Vol. 354, p. 374.
13 Thompson, *Motif-index*, J 1161.3.

The simplest and most drastic solution was to play dumb. However, this could carry attendant supernatural risks – as in the case of a woman who, having pretended to be mute in court, subsequently gave birth to three dumb children.[14]

A more popular ruse was to deny a knowledge of English sufficient to give an accurate testimony. This served three purposes: first, it contributed to delay, as an interpreter would have to be found; second, it provided scope for confusion between the interpreter and the witness, the lawyers and the judge – creating windows of ambiguity which might be profitably exploited without the risk of damning one's soul in perjury; finally, it gave the witness more time (while the interpreter was translating) to consider the questions and frame appropriate responses. According to Waldron, this simple technique was widely used, and Anthony Joyce employed it during the Maamtrasna trials.[15] Desmond MacCabe, in his study of Mayo petty sessions during the early part of the nineteenth century, noted the growing impatience of magistrates with such ploys:

Interpreters were kept at the petty sessions courts in the early 1830s, but it seems that magistrates, later in the decade, listened grudgingly if at all to prosecutions through Irish, and dismissed cases readily if suspicious. At Swinford petty sessions in April 1839, when Pat Gerty objected to giving evidence in a case of trespass 'except in the Irish language', Matthew Gallager, J.P., on being informed by a 'respectable man in court' that 'Gerty could in fact speak English sufficiently well' consigned him to the guard-room.[16]

In 1858, the Irish Court for Crown Cases Reserved were forced to confront this issue in the case of *R.* v. *Burke*.[17] Burke had been accused of raping one Margaret Sheridan. At the trial, a key witness for the defence named Martin Thornton stated that he could not speak English, and was accordingly sworn and examined in Irish, with the assistance of an interpreter. Thornton's statement that he spoke no English was challenged in cross-examination. The trial

14 See below, p. 129.
15 See above, pp. 22–23.
16 MacCabe, 'Magistrates, peasants and the petty sessions courts: Mayo 1823–50', *Cathair na Mart*, v (1985), 45, 49.
17 (1858) 8 Cox CC 44.

judge subsequently allowed the production of two witnesses who said that Thornton had spoken to them in English within the last few days, and had sung a song called 'The heights of Alma' – also in English. The question for the court to resolve was whether such evidence was admissible. Four of the seven judges decided that it was not. Giving the leading judgment for the majority, Christian J felt that the correct time to inquire into the matter would have been when the witness first came to the stand:

... if, when this witness came upon the table, the counsel for the Crown had said, 'We can show that this man is perfectly well able to speak English,' the judge might have heard evidence addressed to himself, to see the form in which this witness should be sworn. I think that course might have been adopted at that stage of the case; but if the time be passed, and the parties wait until the evidence in chief is given before the jury, I think the evidence ought not then to be received.[18]

In any event, he was not convinced that a witness's insistence on being examined in Irish must necessarily be motivated by deceit:

I apprehend it is perfectly possible that the witness was actuated by an honest motive in wishing to be examined in Irish. He may have wished to express himself in the language which he knew best, in which he could most clearly express his thoughts; and is it not easy to imagine that one of us, a person of a rank of life above that of this witness, if giving evidence in an Italian or a French court of justice, would prefer to do so in the English language? – and would we not think it very hard if witnesses were called to convict us of perjury, on the ground that we had been using some words of French or Italian on some previous occasion; and certainly if every lady who sings an Italian song is to be taken on that account to have a perfect knowledge of the Italian language, I can only say that a great number of ladies may very easily find themselves placed in a very unpleasant position indeed.[19]

O'Brien J, in a strong dissenting judgment, felt this approach to be somewhat unrealistic. In his opinion, the existence of a widespread practice of feigning ignorance of English was sufficient to

18 ibid., p. 55.
19 ibid., pp. 54–55.

justify allowing evidence of this type, even at this late stage in the trial:

> I may observe, that the question involved in the case is one of considerable importance as affects the administration of justice in those parts of this country where many persons profess not to speak or understand the English language, and are examined in Irish; and it is especially important with reference to cross-examination, the great value of which arises from the demeanour of the witness, and the hesitation or fairness with which he answers questions unexpected by him, and put suddenly to him, and his demeanour while being so cross-examined is powerful with the jury to judge of the credit which they ought to give to his testimony; and it is plain that the value of this test is very much lessened in the case of a witness having a sufficient knowledge of the English language to understand the questions put by counsel, pretending ignorance of it, and gaining time to consider his answers while the interpreter is going through the useless task of interpreting the question which the witness already perfectly understands.... I cannot conceive anything more serious in those parts of the country where the Irish language is generally spoken, than that a witness should be able, on his own representation, uncontradicted, to place himself at such an advantage over the jury, the counsel, and the judge.[20]

In the fictional world of *The collegians*, Phil Naughten, lacking the wit and intelligence of his sister Poll, feigned ignorance of the English language to great effect. As she had baffled the court with loquacity, so he frustrated them with halting words and the demeanour of a simpleton:

> He approached the table with a fawning smile upon his coarse features, and a helpless, conciliatory glance at every individual around him.
>
> > 'Now we shall have something', said Mr Warner [a magistrate]; 'this fellow has more tractable eye [than his sister, Poll]. Your name is Philip Naughten, is it not?'
>
> The man returned an answer in Irish, which the magistrate cut short in the middle.
>
> > 'Answer me in English, friend. We speak no Irish here. Is your name Philip Naughten?'

20 ibid., pp. 46–47, 52.

'The wisha, vourneen'–

'Come – come – English. Swear him to know whether he does not understand English. Can you speak English, fellow?'

'Not a word, plase your honour.'

A roar of laughter succeeded this escapade, to which the prisoner listened with a wondering and stupid look. Addressing himself in Irish to Mr Cregan [another magistrate], he appeared to make an explanatory speech which was accompanied by a slight expression of indignation.

'What does the fellow say?' asked Mr Warner.

'Why', said Cregan, with a smile, 'he says he will admit that he couldn't *be hung in English before his face,* but he does not know enough of the language to enable him to *tell his story* in English.' [21]

In the folklore archives, a Kerry man recalled a court case between himself and a neighbouring widow. When asked by Wyse, the stipendiary magistrate, to put her case, the widow said she'd no English. The court clerk pointed out that she had completed the form for the summons in English; whereupon Wyse told her to wait outside until such time as she was ready to testify in English. After other cases had been dealt with, she was recalled, and did so testify.[22]

Another option for a reluctant witness was to feign madness. A storyteller from Kerry told of a man called to give evidence at Tralee sessions against others accused of maliciously wounding livestock. Not wishing to incriminate his own people, he brought some porridge into the witness-box with him, and ate a handful for every question put to him. The judge dismissed him as probably mad, and the case against the accused subsequently failed. In an archetypal folk narrative, pretending to be mad is recommended by a lawyer to his client, and is used successfully – not only in court, but also when the lawyer comes to collect his fee. In a version from the border area between Cavan and Meath, a solicitor advised his client to feign lunacy by getting up on a table in the courtroom and singing 'Paudeen O'Rafferty'. She did so, and the charges against her were dropped. When the solicitor

21 Griffin, *The collegians,* pp. 379–80.
22 IFC Ms. Vol. 999, p. 72.

came seeking payment for his services, she simply repeated the act, and he went away empty-handed.[23]

Related to feigned insanity is feigned simplicity. Griffin writes of 'the shrewdness of disguise, the closeness, the affected dulness, the assumed simplicity and all the inimitable subtleties of evasion and wile which an Irish peasant can display when he is made to undergo a scene of judicial scrutiny ...'.[24] One of his characters, Phil Naughten (mentioned already in the context of witnesses who pretended to know no English), wrapped himself in such a cloak of ignorance, meeting all attempts to elicit useful evidence from him with the same simple phrase, repeated in an injured and bewildered tone: 'He could or would admit nothing more than that he was a poor man, who lived by his industry, and that he had rented a small farm from Mr O'Connor, of Crag-beg.'[25]

The persistent repetition of a single phrase was also heard in a story recorded from Bullenstown, Co. Wexford – but not from the witness-box. 'Ould' Tom believed that the son of a woman called Nell was 'stealing' the milk from his goats at night,[26] and duly administered a beating to him when he caught him. This led to an argument between Nell and Tom which ended in violence, and culminated in Nell bringing Tom to court. On the advice of the magistrate's son, Ould Tom stood close to the witness-box, and countered every accusation of Nell's by saying to her, 'You lie, you whore you!' This being too much for any self-respecting woman to bear, Nell eventually lost her temper and flew at him, cursing and swearing. On seeing this unseemly display, the magistrate ordered her to be removed from the court, and the case against Tom was dismissed.[27]

Returning to Maamtrasna: we have noted already that one of the prosecution witnesses, Anthony Joyce, pretended not to know any English. This was not an option for Anthony Philbin, an

---

23 IFC Ms. Vol. 1195, pp. 432–33. This archetype is found internationally, and has been traced back to medieval times. See Uí Ógáin, *Immortal Dan*, p. 127.
24 Griffin, *The collegians*, p. 375.
25 ibid., p. 381.
26 It was widely believed that witches and others had the power to `steal' the milk from an animal by supernatural means ('pishoguery', from the Irish 'piseoga'), so that it could no longer give milk.
27 IFC Ms. Vol. 354, p. 271.

accused man turned informer, who was known to be perfectly fluent. Instead, Philbin pretended to be stupid:

In general, Philbin was quite frank and outcoming when confronted with any of the Crown counsel. But, when the Defence faced him, he pretended to be slow-witted and uncomprehending and spoke in a deliberately low voice. He was not the only one to adopt this ploy. His brother-in-law, Tom Casey, later also had to be frequently asked to speak up, because his mumbled replies were not audible to the Jurors or the Judge.[28]

KINSHIP AND COMMUNITY

The importance of clan and family in rural Irish life cannot be overestimated. It seems that in many cases, loyalty to kin was placed above loyalty to the truth and to justice. In a situation where to tell the truth could hurt one's brother, sister or close neighbour, perjury was often seen as the lesser of two evils. This penchant for placing the welfare of one's kin above the sanctity of an oath was greeted with astonishment and no little sarcasm by some writers. Inglis related it in particular to faction fighting – a form of recreational violence between families and clans which formed an integral part of Irish social life in the early nineteenth century. His account of this activity and its legal aftermath approaches the language of farce, though he himself clearly believes it to be no laughing matter:

The English murder is a private act, perpetrated by some ruffian for the sake of gain: the Irish homicide has been committed for no reason at all; and not by one cold-blooded ruffian, but by a crowd of demi-barbarians, who meet for the purpose of fighting; and who have no other reason for fighting, than because one half of the number are called O'Sullivan, and the other O' something else: so that when a manslaughter is to be presented at an Irish assizes the case does not bring up merely the accused and his one or two witnesses, but it brings up half the 'boys' in the county who bear the same name as the accused; and as many more, of the same name as the man who was killed – every one of the former, ready to kiss the book, and swear that the boy accused of the homicide, never lifted a stone, or was seen in a 'scrimmage' in his days; and every one of the

28 Waldron, *Maamtrasna*, p. 69.

latter as ready to swear, that the boy that was killed was the most peacable boy that ever bore his name, and that he was killed for no reason at all.[29]

Further on, he concluded that 'To save a relative from punishment, or to punish anyone who has injured a relation, an Irish peasant will swear anything.'[30] Writing on the Aran islands, Synge noted that reliable evidence was, by and large, impossible to get from the islanders, who held the bonds of kinship to be 'more sacred than the claims of abstract truth'.[31]

In his 'Essay on Irish swearing', Carleton damns the archetypal Irish peasant with excessive praise for his ability in swearing alibis for such of his relations as are in need of one:

[There] is the one department of oath-making in which he stands unrivalled and unapproachable.... There is where he shines, where his oath, instead of being a mere matter of fact or opinion, rises up into the dignity of epic narrative, containing within itself all the complexity of machinery, harmony of parts, and fertility of invention, by which your true epic should be characterised.... Put him forward to prove an alibi for his fourteenth or fifteenth cousin, and you will be gratified by the pomp, pride and circumstance of true swearing.[32]

Healy noted two types of manufactured alibi which were so popular in Munster as to have gained nicknames:

A 'Kerry alibi' was a phrase.... Its essence was that the story was true in every respect except one: the date.... A 'Tipperary alibi' was a more elaborate affair than the Kerry kind. When the Crown witnesses had told their story at petty sessions, a mass of evidence was prepared in respect of each one of them to prove that he, the Crown witness, was somewhere else than the place he had sworn to on the day of the crime.[33]

A story from Limerick concerns a man popularly believed to have murdered his wife. His whole family were arrested on suspicion.

29 Inglis, *Ireland in 1834*, pp. 279–80.
30 ibid., p. 284.
31 Synge, *Aran islands*, p. 64.
32 Carleton, *Traits and stories*, 2nd series, i, 268.
33 Healy, *Old Munster circuit*, pp. 168, 170.

Unfortunately, they were all placed in the one cell, with the result that, by the time the morning of the hearing came, their alibis had been perfectly harmonised. The case ended without anyone being found guilty. The storyteller concluded that 'the police made the great mistake of treating the people of the district as backward. They were backward all right but they were shrewd.'[34]

While creative perjury on behalf of friends and relatives seems to have been common, it was not universal. There is a contrasting strand of rural wisdom which advocated avoidance of court cases and disputes wherever possible. One source said, 'I knew of people to pass things by and shut their eyes afraid they'd be brought as a witness…. A wise man never finds a dead man.'[35] Such reticence seems to have been the ruination of one Gillick, wrongly convicted of having taken part in a violent gang attack on a neighbour: 'Hundreds could swear he wasn't there at all, but they didn't turn up at the court to give evidence.'[36] In Waldron's initial description of Myles Joyce, one of those hanged for the Maamtrasna murders, he tells us that

Myles had the peasant's natural suspicion about Law and Courts. This was added to because many years previously, as a local tradition has it, Myles on a bona fide mission of mercy for a neighbour had unwittingly become embroiled as a witness in a tragic case in which a man called Leyden was charged with the murder of his wife. Myles' memories of Court hearings had not been particularly happy.[37]

In close-knit communities, testimony on oath against a neighbour or relation could be treated as a hostile act – regardless of whether the evidence given was true or not.[38] This could lead to an escalation of existing feuds, or the creation of new ones, with potentially devastating consequences for the stability of the community. The giving of testimony against a party, though not motivated by any malice or ill-feeling, could be treated by that

---

34 IFC Ms. Vol. 1210, p. 21.
35 IFC Ms. Vol. 1195, p. 371.
36 IFC Ms. Vol. 1196, pp. 414–15.
37 Waldron, *Maamtrasna*, p. 108.
38 See K. Mann, *Law in colonial Africa* (London 1991), p. 208.

party as a declaration of war – thus forcing the unfortunate witness to take sides in an expanded conflict. Many felt this was a risk to be avoided at all costs. The fear of becoming inadvertently involved in someone else's dispute has lasted in isolated rural communities to this day, as Curtin found when studying dispute resolution in a small Mayo village. A long-running argument over a right of way found expression in sporadic outbursts of violence, before eventually leading to litigation. Throughout the course of the dispute, Curtin notes that,

Apart from the priest, who lives in the town, and a few of the villagers who set themselves up as 'formal' mediators, a number of villagers had, from time to time, suggested to the disputants that they had little to gain from continuing the conflict. None however allied themselves with either side and none were willing to become directly involved.[39]

A disinclination to testify in court could also be prompted by the risk of being tagged 'an informer' – probably the worst insult in the vocabulary of rural eighteenth- and nineteenth-century Ireland.[40]

One Kerry witness found a rather eloquent solution to this predicament. He was reckoned to know who had stolen a particular quantity of timber, and was summoned to appear at a hearing before the local landlord. Not wishing to be seen accusing others, yet unwilling to lie under oath, he conceived the idea of swearing

---

39 Chris Curtin, 'Social order, interpersonal relations and disputes in a west of Ireland community', in M. Tomlinson (ed.), *Whose law and order?* (Belfast, 1988), pp. 84–85.

40 The greatest scorn of the Irish peasant was reserved for 'political' informers – as evinced by this passage from *Glenanaar* (Dublin, 1989), by Canon P. Sheehan (Glenanaar was first published in 1905):

> The awful stain goes down from generation to generation, and their children and children's children are the pariahs with whom no man will willingly converse with, and with whom any alliance, particularly of marriage, is regarded as treasonable and dishonourable to the last degree. (p. 71)

The naming of people as informers, or potential informers has occasionally surfaced in defamation actions before the courts: for instance, *Mawe* v. *Pigott* (1869) IR 4 CL 54, and more recently, *Berry* v. *Irish Times Ltd* [1973] IR 368.

In the eighteenth and nineteenth centuries, a measure of the ire directed at political informers was also directed towards those who accused people of lesser offences, unrelated to matters of politics or land agitation.

on a prayerbook, prior to his appearance in court, not to give sworn evidence against anyone that day. When the case came up for hearing, he explained that he was bound to silence in this way, and this resulted in all the suspects being released for lack of evidence.[41] Another Kerry man told of how his great-grandfather was returning from Dingle with two relations. A fight broke out between his two companions, which led in due course to a court case. The speaker's great-grandfather was called as a witness, but being reluctant to swear against a relative, refused to take the oath. As a result, the judge ordered that he join his relatives in gaol.[42]

One could also avoid testifying by demonstrating one's own unreliability as a witness. This was done by a man named McCabe, who swore assiduously against those accused in a case, then deliberately destroyed his testimony by finishing, 'If that doesn't hang them, I'll swear as much more.'[43] A labourer from the Leitrim-Cavan border told a story of a man reluctant to give evidence who stood up and asked the judge if another witness could give his evidence first. When asked why, he replied, 'He's a decent, respectable man, and he has a better education than me. And whatever he swears I'll swear the same.' The judge was forced to dismiss him from the courtroom.[44]

The reluctance to be seen to be acting against one's neighbour occasionally caused people to try and avoid jury service, although some Cavan informants did not recall widespread objections in their local area to serving on juries.[45] In the Limerick story of an accused family and their alibi, referred to above, the jury consisted of locals, none of whom wished to be on it. One of their number, a man named Mulvihill, stood up in court and suggested that the four suspects be hanged before the case proceeded. This was deemed sufficient proof of his unreliability as a juror, and he was dismissed from the case – which of course was his aim.[46]

---

41 IFC Ms. Vol. 715, p. 146.
42 IFC Ms. Vol. 534, p. 345.
43 IFC Ms. Vol. 715, p. 146; Vol. 1196, p. 65.
44 IFC Ms. Vol. 1197, p. 180; Vol. 1196, pp. 65–66.
45 IFC Ms. Vol. 1196, p. 8; Vol. 1195, p. 496.
46 IFC Ms. Vol. 1210, p. 21.

Another Limerick tale concerned a Sinn Féin court, presided over by a Father O'Riordan. It was said that everyone tried to avoid jury duty on it; one person going so far as to pretend to be a fool.[47]

---

47 IFC Ms. Vol. 1194, p. 562. The Sinn Féin courts, also known as Dáil courts, came into existence around the time of the setting up of the first Dáil, following the secession of Sinn Féin MPs from Westminster in 1918. They arose initially as a spontaneous response to outbreaks of agrarian violence in the west of Ireland, and were given a formal structure by the Dáil in 1920. The advent of civil war led to the collapse of the system, and it was replaced in 1924 by new structures, as set out in the Courts of Justice Act of that year. For an account of the history of Sinn Féin courts, see Mary Kotsonouris, *Retreat from revolution: the Dáil courts, 1920–1924* (Dublin, 1994).

CHAPTER SIX

Law and the supernatural

ALLUSIONS TO A supernatural world coexistent with, and occasionally breaking into, the physical realm, are a near-constant feature of Irish folklore. Blessings, curses, omens and portents; witches, fairies, ghosts and apparitions; such occult phenomena were, if the evidence of our oral folk culture is to be believed, a recognised and accepted part of Irish rural life in the eighteenth and nineteenth centuries. Many writers have dealt with the subject of peasant superstition and fear of the supernatural; one thinks of Sir William Wilde's *Irish popular superstitions*, Ó Catháin's *Irish life and lore*, O'Farrell's *Superstitions of Irish country people*, Power's *The book of Irish curses*, and Ó Súilleabháin's *Irish folk custom and belief*, among others. The fictional works of Carleton, Griffin and the Banim brothers are also permeated with references to paranormal events and otherworldly powers. When one looks at this in the context of law, an immediate point of contact between the legal and supernatural worlds comes to mind: the use of oaths to combat lying and falsehood. The oath has long played a significant role in legal and quasi-legal proceedings around the world; finding its way into the Hebraic and Babylonian codes, and cropping up in studies of primitive tribes in Africa, Asia and the Americas by Gluckman, Hoebel and others. The effectiveness with which it has been employed in so many diverse cultures is in large part due to the supernatural or divine power which it is invariably believed to possess. In dealing with this topic therefore I propose to concentrate primarily on the use of oaths – in legal and non-legal disputes – before turning briefly to examine some other superstitious beliefs which have accompanied matters pertaining to law.

106

OATHS AND SWEARING

Ireland presents a confusing image when it comes to the importance and sacredness of oaths amongst ordinary people. Dire warnings as to the evil consequences of perjury clash with statements that lying under oath was 'as common as grass'. One Cavan informant could say that 'There was plenty of false swearing long ago – any amount of it' – and follow that with an assertion that 'A perjurer was one of the lowest descriptions of a man. He was reckoned the next step to the informer'[1] – hardly credible if perjury was as common as he suggests. People are presented, on the one hand, as being reluctant to swear an oath under any circumstances, and on the other, as being willing to swear anything to help a neighbour or a kinsman. A partial explanation for these inconsistencies may lie in the inherent weaknesses of folklore material as an historical source: as we've said before, it must be remembered that general statements may in fact only relate to particular localities, times, or classes of people. In any analysis which bases itself upon sources of this type, there remains an extent to which confusion must exist – the folk picture of the past, like any other picture, is necessarily incomplete.

Having attended sessions at the court in Ennis, Co. Clare, in 1834, Inglis reported rather dramatically that 'If positive falsehood will serve the end, it is unhesitatingly resorted to; and as for telling the whole truth, I saw no one instance of it.'[2] Alexis de Tocqueville was even more blunt, saying, 'there is not a country where it is more difficult to obtain the truth from a man.'[3] Maurice Healy, in seeking to demonstrate the difference between Irish and English witnesses, told a story of a case in which his father was counsel, which came up for trial in England before Mr Justice Darling:

The point at issue was the identity of a valuable picture, and hosts of witnesses, many of them humble Irish folk, were examined on either side. One of these Irishmen, who had tuned his harp to the romantic air

1 IFC Ms. Vol. 1196, p. 429.
2 Inglis, *Ireland in 1834*, p. 292.
3 de Tocqueville, *Journey in Ireland*, p. 21.

of his own County Court, was a shock to a judge of pedestrian imagination. Darling at last turned to him sternly and said: 'Tell me, in your
country what happens to a witness who does not tell the truth?' 'Begor,
me Lord', replied the Irishman, with a candour that disarmed all
criticism, 'I think his side usually wins!'[4]

A Cavan farmer said that 'Unless you could swear white was black
and black was white you mightn't be entering into a court. Whoever
could swear best won his case. Unless you were prepared to swear
anything to win, you wouldn't win',[5] implying that creative testimony reaped more awards than mere truth-telling. His view was
echoed by a man from Kerry, albeit with the proviso that he was
referring to 'the olden days': 'Is mó leabhair a tugtar bun os cionn
i gcúirteanna, [go] mórmhór sa tseanshaol – is dócha ná raibh
daoine comh dea-chreidmheach agus táid siad anois.'[6]

Carleton devoted an entire essay to the phenomenon of oath-
swearing in his *Traits and stories of the Irish peasantry*. He suggested that Irish reverence for the oath in court was destroyed by
the lack of ceremony surrounding it, and by the indifferent tone
in which it was usually put to the witness:

To many of the uninitiated Irish an oath is a solemn, to some, an awful
thing. Of this wholesome reverence for its sanction, two or three testi-
monies in a court usually cure them. The indifferent, business-like
manner in which the oaths are put, the sing-song tone of voice, the rapid
utterance of the words, give to this solemn act an appearance of excellent
burlesque, which ultimately renders the whole proceedings remarkable
for the absence of truth and reality; but, at the same time, gives them
unquestionable merit as a dramatic representation, abounding with
fiction, well related, and ably acted.[7]

This complaint was not a new one; nor was it confined to Ireland.
Keith Thomas, in his *Religion and the decline of magic*, records the

---

4   Healy, *Old Munster circuit*, p. 92.
5   IFC Ms. Vol. 1197, p. 13.
6   'Many false oaths were taken in court, especially in the olden days – I
    suppose that people weren't as pious as they are now.' IFC Ms. Vol. 1000,
    p. 142. See also above, chapter 5.
7   Carleton, *Traits and stories*, 2nd series, i, 276–77.

views of an early seventeenth-century Puritan on the increasing incidence of perjury in England, and the corresponding decrease in reverence for the oath, as people saw neighbours and acquaintances perjuring themselves while God seemingly stood by and did nothing:

How many oaths are ministered daily to churchwardens, constables, jurors and witnesses, at every assize and sessions, in every court, baron and leet, in every commission ... and no man regardeth them any more than the taking up of a straw; they think it is no more than the laying on the hand and the kissing of the book. 'Tush', thinks every man, 'the taking of these oaths is a matter of nothing; all my neighbours have taken them before me, and made no reckoning of them.'[8]

Whatever about the reverence accorded to the oath in the atmosphere of a court, swearing did form an important part of most forms of non-legal dispute settlement. De Latocnaye, for instance, mentions a black bell, kept in a chapel on the summit of Croagh Patrick:[9] 'It is used as a thing to swear on in legal matters, and no-one will dare perjure himself on it. They ... believe that the devil will carry them off immediately if they dare to affirm on it anything that is not true.'[10] Another narrative concerns one Padraic Walshe, whose clothes were stolen from his washing line. He responded by threatening publicly to go up to a nearby monastery and swear, on a skull kept there, against those whom he believed to be responsible for the crime. Before he got to carry out this threat, the clothes were returned.[11]

I refer elsewhere in this work to accounts of a customary court for settling claims relating to stray sheep, which operated in Co. Mayo.[12] Part of the procedure of this court involved witnesses being sworn on a book – 'any old book at all would do – preferably a prayer book'. The court was said to have continued near

---

8 Keith Thomas, *Religion and the decline of magic* (Harmondsworth, 1973), p. 77.
9 A mountain in Co. Mayo, and one of the most famous Christian pilgrimage sites in Ireland.
10 de Latocnaye, *A Frenchman's walk through Ireland, 1796–1797*, p. 174.
11 IFC Ms. Vol. 195, p. 71.
12 See below, pp. 155–56.

Erris until the 1950s. Another simpler procedure from the same area also involved the use of oaths:

When quarrelling persons accused each other as they often did of having committed some crime such as sheep stealing or where perhaps the opprobrium of spying or giving information to the authorities was alleged, it was usual for the injured party to come to the house of the accuser with a book and on his or her knees the person swore by the book in protestation of his innocence. If possible the person would be prevented from giving the oath on the knees, as it was said, if such a person was wrongfully accused, the evil or wrath of the malicious libel, if it were one, would fall on the person guilty of the defamation. But if the person swore his innocence in a standing position there was a modification of the result.[13]

At an even more basic level, an oath could be the means of putting an end to rumour by way of a public proclamation of innocence – this was often done in front of a congregation after mass. One example from Mayo tells of a man generally believed to have been the father of a child born out of wedlock to a young girl. On a Sunday, the man in question entered the church carrying a skull in a handkerchief, and there swore upon the skull that he was not the father. This oath was reckoned to be serious, and he was believed.[14] The town of Cleggan (from the Irish, 'cloigeann', meaning skull or head), Co. Galway, received its name from a famous skull (supposedly belonging to a saint) which was used for swearing on. It was said that anyone who lied on it would see its reflection in every drink they had from then on – a fairly mild punishment, compared to those associated with some other relics.[15] The county of Cavan was also familiar with the custom of taking oaths upon a skull: one man recalled that 'In most cases there was an old building in a graveyard; there would be a niche in it, and the skull that they swore on would be left in it, and they'd go for it when they'd be going to hold a court.'[16]

13 IFC Ms. Vol. 1242, p. 576.
14 IFC Ms. Vol. 804, p. 306; Vol. 805, p. 242.
15 IFC Ms. Vol. 1242, p. 576.
16 IFC Ms. Vol. 1196, p. 428.

Perhaps the most bizarre story involving this custom is that of a woman who was alleged to have committed a serious wrong 'a good many years ago'. She offered to swear on the skull of 'that person' (possibly the victim of the alleged wrong), and proceeded to go to the grave and dig up the skull. On her way home, she stopped overnight at a friend's house and buried the skull outside. That night there was a ferocious thunderstorm, in the midst of which the ground opened up and went down into the sea, bringing the skull with it. The storyteller gave no suggestions as to what meaning or moral should be drawn from this strange sequence of events.[17]

Other objects said to have been employed at one time or another for the purpose of oath-swearing include bibles, mass vestments, holy water, and prayer books (or failing that, a book of any sort). In Co. Kilkenny, it was reported in 1839 that persons accused of theft were asked to drink a glass of water from a certain well, in the belief that anyone who did so, having perjured themselves, would be punished by having their mouth leave its proper place and take up residence under their left ear. From Cork and Donegal comes mention of a special collar known as *An Iodh Morainn*, which was placed around the neck of the person swearing, and was believed to choke or decapitate would-be perjurers.[18] This is in fact a reference to an ancient Irish legend. Morann was a mythical Irish judge, celebrated for his wisdom. According to Ó hÓgáin,

Both early and late sources tell of the 'sín' or 'íodh' of Morann. This was the remnant of his caul,[19] which remained around his neck, and if ever he was beginning to give a wrong judgment it would tighten on him and thus lead him to revise his decision. A development of this states that he used to place it on the neck of an accused person, and that it would choke the guilty but spare the innocent.[20]

17 IFC Ms. Vol. 1190, p. 449.
18 IFC Ms. Vol. 186, p. 370.
19 'Caul: the amnion or inner membrane inclosing the foetus before birth; *esp.* This or a portion of it sometimes enveloping the head of the child at birth, superstitiously regarded as of good omen, and supposed to be a preservative against drowning.' (*OED*, 2nd ed., Oxford, 1989.)
20 Daithí Ó hÓgáin, *Myth, legend and romance: an encyclopaedia of the Irish folk tradition* (London, 1990), p. 306.

In Cavan, use was made of a bishop's staff, known as a 'bauhil'.[21] The oath was taken while holding the staff in the right hand, and if the person lied, their mouth would turn sideways.[22] One man said his grandfather had seen it also being used by the Ribbonmen to swear in new members.[23] 'He said it had a distorted face on it.... it was made of wood. He was either told or understood that anyone that took a false oath on it would get a twisted mouth.' Anyone who wished to use it had to borrow it from the house in which it was kept, leaving some form of guarantee that it would be returned.

With regard to the use of mass vestments and other items belonging to the church, it is worth noting that their use implies a clergy who not merely tolerated such superstitious practices, but actively supported them. The position of the church hierarchy on the matter was quite clear: from the seventeenth century onwards, the combining of religious belief with superstitious practice was roundly condemned. But Connolly suggests that some of the ordinary priests and curates adopted a more lenient attitude to such customs. He cites amongst other examples the custodian of a crozier in Taughboy, Co. Galway, which was used frequently for swearing on: afterwards, it was his job to return it and prepare it for church use again by getting the priest to reconsecrate it. However, some time before 1838 it seems that a new parish priest refused to perform the act of reconsecration, and publicly condemned the practice of swearing on the crozier in the first place.[24]

The use of oaths to formally declare one's innocence forms the centrepiece of William Carleton's short story, 'The horse-stealers'. The story is worth examining in some detail, as it is an extraordinarily rich source of information and insight into the folk

---

21 In Irish, *bachall*, meaning staff or crozier.
22 IFC Ms. Vol. 1196, p. 4
23 IFC Ms Vol. 1196, p. 401. The secret society known as the Ribbonmen was born out of sectarian strife in Ulster at the turn of the nineteenth century, but very quickly became associated with agrarian violence. As agrarian unrest spread throughout Ireland, Ribbonism became a generic term for any secret society concerned with land reform. See Joseph Lee, 'The Ribbonmen', in T.D. Williams (ed.), *Secret societies in Ireland* (Dublin, 1973), p. 26.
24 Connolly, *Priests and people*, pp. 112–13.

1 'The trial'

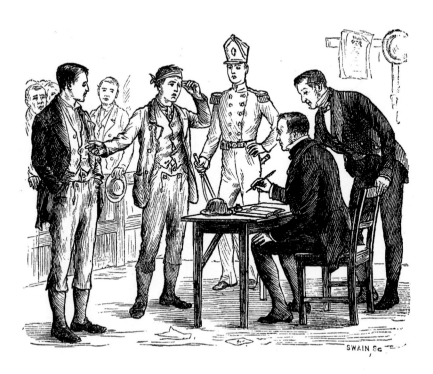

2 'Petty sessions, Roundstone, Co. Galway – 1'

3 'Petty sessions,
  Roundstone,
  Co. Galway – 2'

4 'In the courthouse,
  Waterford'

5   William Carleton in old age

6   Carleton's cottage, near Clogher, Co. Tyrone

7 'Preparing for examination'

8 'God of Heaven an' earth! have I murdered my daughter': the fatal
last scene in Carleton's story, 'The horse-stealers'

10 Gerald Griffin

11 Poster advertising a production of Boucicault's
'The Colleen Bawn'

12 Prionnsias de Búrca, folklore collector

coimisiún béaloideasa éireann

connтae _na zaillime_   barúntaċt _Ros_
paróiste _Ros_

Ainm an Sgriobnóra _Proinn sias de Búrca_

Seolad an Sgriobnóra _Core-na-mónad Clár Cloinne Muiris_
Co. na Zaillime

Do repiobar rior an _sgéal_ ro ar an _1-3-1943_

ó béal-aitrir _Pádraig ó Súilleabáin_

Aor _78_ gairm beata _feilméaraí_ atá in a comnuí

i mbaile fearainn _Baile an Tobair_

agur a raoluiod agur a tógad i _mbaile an Tobair_

Do cuala ré (rí) ar _sgéal_ roblianta ólian ó rin ona _Seán_
ua Duinió (Aor an uair rin.) a bí in a comnuí an uair rin
i _mbaile an Tobair_

𝑓 = adeir
ꝼ = adubairt.

13 Specimen archival record, Irish Folklore Commission

attitude towards swearing and the supernatural. The action revolves around the inhabitants of Carnmore – 'one of those small villages that are to be found in the outskirts of many parishes in Ireland'.[25] With the arrival of two brothers, Anthony and Denis Meehan, to live in the area came a spate of well-organised thefts. The brothers were suspected, but no direct evidence could be found to incriminate them. Matters finally came to a head with the daring robbery of a horse from the wealthy Cassidy family:

When a fortnight or so had elapsed, and no circumstances transpired that might lead to discovery, the neighbours, including those who had principally suffered by the robberies, determined to meet upon a certain day at Cassidy's house, for the purpose of clearing themselves, on oath, of the imputation thrown out against some of them, as accomplices in the thefts.[26]

To ensure solemnity in the ceremony, the local parish priest, his curate and the local magistrate were invited to preside over it. The meeting was then announced from the pulpit on the following Sunday:

In fact, the intended meeting, and the object of it, were already notorious; and much conversation was held upon its probable result, and the measures which might be taken against those who should refuse to swear. Of the latter description there was but one opinion, which was that their refusal in such a case would be tantamount to guilt.[27]

The oath itself was drawn up by the priest and his curate, 'who, as they knew the reservations and evasions commonest among such characters, had ingeniously contrived not to leave a single loophole through which the consciences of those who belonged to this worthy fraternity might escape.'[28]

The process of swearing went smoothly enough; the oath was taken while holding the 'law bible' (as it was somewhat contemptuously referred to by the people). Carleton does not make clear

25 Carleton, *Traits and stories,* 2nd series, i, 153.
26 ibid., p. 173.
27 ibid., p. 174.
28 ibid., p. 175.

whether by the 'law bible' was meant the Protestant rather than Catholic version of scripture, or whether it referred to the actual copy which was kept in court. On completion of the oath, the book was to be kissed. Innocent or not, a number of those present sought to kiss their thumb or the air rather than the book itself – owing to a form of superstitious legalism which believed the oath to be valid only if the physical conditions of its swearing, i.e. the actual kissing of the book, were carried out to the letter.

The ceremony was at length completed, the guilty parties confidently swearing their innocence along with all the others. Then, however, events took a dramatic turn, as the priests began to increase the supernatural pressure on any perjurers:

Just at this moment, a person from Cassidy's laid upon the table a small box covered with a thick black cloth; and our readers will be surprised to hear, that if fire had come down visibly from heaven, greater awe and fear could not have been struck into their hearts, or depicted on their countenances.... 'Let', said the curate, 'none of those who have sworn depart ... until they once more clear themselves upon this', and as he spoke, he held it up – 'behold!' said he, 'and tremble – behold *The Donagh!!!*'[29]

The sudden unveiling of this artefact (the exact nature and provenance of which is regrettably not given by the author) had an immediate and spectacular effect on the audience. Those who had sworn already 'appeared ready to sink into the earth ... many of them became almost unable to stand; and altogether, the state of trepidation and terror in which they stood, was strikingly wild and extraordinary.'[30] Lest there was anyone there who did not feel such terror, the curate then continued with an outline of the Donagh's power:

29 ibid., p. 197. The *Donagh* is probably to be identified with the Irish *domhnach*, one of the meanings of which is 'shrine or gospel-case': Royal Irish Academy, *Dictionary of the Irish language*, s.v. 'domhnach' (c). See, too, the lengthy footnote appended by Carleton to 'The horse-stealers' in the 1844 edition of *Traits and stories*, which combined the two series already published in one two-volume set, with additional illustrations and footnotes (ii, 401–06).

30 Carleton, *Traits and stories*, 2nd series, i, 198.

Who has ever been known to swear falsely upon the Donagh, without being visited by a tremendous punishment, either on the spot, or in twenty-four hours after his perjury! ... Sudden death, madness, paralysis, self-destruction, or the murder of some one dear to them, are the marks by which perjury upon the Donagh is known and visited.[31]

The evil consequences were said not to be for the perjurer alone: 'for if this grievous sin be committed, a heavy punishment will fall, not only upon you, but upon the parish in which it occurs!'[32]

Carleton's intent in this story was to expose the superstitious double standards of men and women who would perjure themselves on the word of God without qualm, yet baulked at swearing falsely upon religious artefacts or relics such as the Donagh. With his enthusiastic conversion to Protestantism, Carleton himself professed to have left all superstition behind; but one is tempted to find some vestige of belief in the conclusion of this story, as the curate's prophecy concerning the vengeance of the Donagh on liars is fulfilled. Anthony Meehan, the fearsome leader of the horse-stealing gang, and the real villain of the piece, swears his innocence on the Donagh. His weak-willed brother Denis cannot bring himself to do so, and in an attempt to silence Denis before he blurts out the truth, Anthony accidentally shoots his own daughter – the one person in the world he really cared for. Thus the Donagh claims its victim, and popular belief in its power is reinforced.

I have mentioned already that in swearing on the bible, many took great care to avoid kissing the book itself, hoping in this way to avoid the supernatural sanction of the oath. A moment of comic relief from the tension of Carleton's story is provided when one Jem Hartigan is caught kissing his thumb rather than the bible. When this is pointed out to him, he responds with a volley of *informal* oaths: 'Not kiss it, your honour? Why, by this staff in my hand, if ever a man kissed – I'd give my oath, an' be the five crasses, I kissed it as sure as —.'[33] When made to repeat the procedure, he kisses neither his thumb nor the book, but this time avoids detection.

31 ibid.
32 ibid., p. 199.
33 ibid., p. 193.

Carleton returns to the topic of thumb-kissing in his 'Essay on Irish swearing'. He declares of the typical Irish 'Paddy' that

It would be impossible for him in many cases to meet the perplexities of a cross-examination so cleverly as he does, if he did not believe that he had, by kissing his thumb instead of the book, actually taken no oath, and consequently given to himself a wider range of action.[34]

In Griffin's *The collegians*, Poll Naughten's failure to kiss the book is suspected, and she is made to repeat the process.[35]

Attending the Ennis assizes, Henry Inglis noted that great importance was attached to kissing the book: witnesses had to be watched carefully to make sure they were not kissing their thumb instead.[36] In 1844, having visited Irish courtrooms, James Johnson was moved to suggest, sardonically, a new form of oath, running as follows:

Remember, Witness! that, in swearing by the Holy Evangelist, you are to take most especial care, *not* to kiss the Cross that is on the book, but your thumb that is on the Cross – and then you are *neither* to tell the whole truth, nor any part of the truth, so help you Bob.[37]

Alexis de Tocqueville also found evidence that the mechanics of swearing were regarded as more important than the spirit in which the oath was sworn. At the Kilkenny assizes, he witnessed the hearing of a case between a farmer and a hired hand:

A farmer dismisses his servant. The latter presents himself at his house the following night, a Bible in one hand and a pistol in the other and forces him to swear an oath that he will take him back into his service. If an individual has taken a similar oath and fails to keep it, the one who made him swear it believes himself authorised to kill him.... What a singular mixture of religion and wickedness. Of respect for the sanctity of an oath, which forms the foundation of every society, and of contempt for all the laws of society![38]

34 Carleton, *Traits and stories*, 2nd series, i, 277.
35 Griffin, *The collegians*, pp. 376–77.
36 Inglis, *Ireland in 1834*, pp. 290–91.
37 Johnson, *A tour in Ireland*, pp. 275–79.
38 de Tocqueville, *Journey in Ireland*, pp. 69–70.

But to return once more to 'The horse-stealers'. The description of the crowd's reaction to the practice of thumb-kissing is in itself instructive; being a mix of laughter on the one hand, and solemn, sober disapproval on the other:

The detections of thumb-kissing were received by those who had already sworn, and by several in the outward crowd, with much mirth. It is but justice, however, to many of those assembled to state, that they appeared to entertain a serious opinion of the nature of the ceremony, and no small degree of abhorrence against those who seemed to trifle with the solemnity of an oath.[39]

Carleton seems to think that thumb-kissing and similar tricks are indicators of a lack of reverence towards the oath being sworn; in fact, the opposite is the case. If the consequences of perjury were not feared, there would be no reason to attempt such evasive measures. What such tricks do indicate is a lack of reverence for truth *per se*. Lying, or being creative with the truth, is not a problem, as long as the possibility of supernatural punishment can be avoided. Hence the need to have the full supernatural authority of the Church behind the ceremony, and hence the various attempts to circumvent that authority and nullify the evil magical effects of lying, much as children today might cross their fingers behind their back in the belief that this action nullifies a spoken promise. Fear of God and the devil, rather than respect for truth, is the ruling motivation. Certain comments in the folklore archives support this: '[People were] very much afraid of the spiritual consequences of taking a false oath which they regarded as the most heinous crime any person could be guilty of';[40] 'In those days people had extreme regard and reverence for the sanctity of an oath even at ... private courts ... [Perjury was] not less heinous than murder itself';[41] 'There was nothing thought of a perjurer – he wasn't wanted in any decent society. A false oath was looked on as a crime against God and man, and the people look on it the

39 Carleton, *Traits and stories*, 2nd series, i, 195.
40 IFC Ms. Vol. 1244, p. 344.
41 IFC Ms. Vol. 1242, p. 576.

same way still.'[42] Other comments regarding perjury were that it 'was looked on as degrading and a great crime';[43] and perjurers were said to be 'held in much the same abhorrence as a person that was actually excommunicated'.[44]

The fear or dislike of taking an oath in ceremonial or 'official' circumstances crops up in a story told by Peig Sayers, the renowned Blasket islands storyteller. It seems that the famous Kerry poet Aogán Ó Rathaille was once asked to appear in court as a witness for a defendant farmer. He refused to take the court oath, but 'swore' in his own fashion, in the defendant's favour. Peig tells us that his informal testimony was accepted, and the farmer won his case.[45] Possibly Ó Rathaille agreed with the man from Meath who told a folklore collector that 'Above all things, the people didn't like swearing.... They reckoned it as sinful, and that it wasn't lucky ...'.[46]

OTHER SUPERSTITIONS

Murder

Apart from oaths and swearing, there are other areas of the law that have associations with certain superstitious beliefs and practices. One is that of unresolved crimes, especially murder. In cases where the legal process failed to identify the guilty party, magic or superstition could often fill the gap and persuade people that they had found a culprit. A widely held belief in nineteenth-century rural Ireland was that the corpse of a murdered person would bleed in the presence of the murderer.[47] It even surfaces in the law reports, being mentioned in an Irish criminal case called *The King* v. *Gibney,* a case heard in November 1822.[48] A nine-

---

42 IFC Ms. Vol. 1196, p. 261.
43 IFC Ms. Vol. 1196, p. 96.
44 IFC Ms. Vol. 1197, p. 75.
45 IFC Ms. Vol. 859, p. 513.
46 IFC Ms. Vol. 1195, p. 371.
47 IFC Ms. Vol. 1196, p. 127.
48 Robert Jebb, *Cases, chiefly relating to the criminal and presentment law, reserved for consideration and decided by the twelve judges of Ireland, May 1822–Nov. 1840* (Dublin, 1841), p. 15.

month-old girl had been found drowned in a bog-hole in County Cavan. Gibney, the father of the child, was arrested on suspicion of murder. Having first brought him before a magistrate, two police constables then brought Gibney to the field where the body of his daughter lay. One of the constables, Thomas Lennon, said that this was in order that Gibney could identify the body as that of his daughter. The other, Arthur Foster, said that 'the prisoner was brought to the body in the hope that his conscience might strike him'. Lennon admitted that he 'had heard of a superstitious notion prevailing among country people as to the effect of a murderer touching the body of the person murdered.... if the murderer touches the body of the person he has killed, the nose of the deceased will bleed'.

On arriving at the field where the victim lay, they found a large group of people gathered there, some of whom were openly accusing Gibney of murder, saying he would hang for it. Lennon told the court that one of those present, in particular a Dr Fitzpatrick, 'was anxious that the prisoner should touch the body'.

... he [Gibney] was brought to the body and touched it; the people were about him, and talking on the subject of murder. After he [Lennon] had brought away the prisoner, and had proceeded about a quarter of a mile towards the gaol, witness [Lennon] said to him [Gibney], 'You must be a very unhappy boy to have murdered your own child, if it be the case.' The prisoner was crying very severely. Witness then said, 'Did you kill the child?' The prisoner then said he had done so....[49]

The issue which came before the court was whether this confession was admissible, given the circumstances which had led to it. In the end, the court held that it was. Inadmissibility was held to be dependent on threats of a temporal nature having been made towards the accused; in this case, 'any terror that might have been excited was as to what might happen in the next world'.[50]

According to Jarlath Waldron, the 'bleeding corpse' phenomenon was also referred to by George Orme Malley, counsel for Myles Joyce during the Maamtrasna murder trials:

49 ibid., p. 16.
50 ibid., p. 19.

Malley dwelt for some time on the implausibility of Myles wanting to kill his own kinsman, and then to have the gall to go to the Wake. He referred to a current superstition. 'I believe there is not a peasant in the land who is not familiar with it – that if you approach the corpse which your hand violated, possibly blood may start from the re-opened wound. That poor peasant, uneducated as he is, if he were guilty, he would have fled from the law.'[51]

During the funeral of an elderly couple who had been murdered at Killinkere, Co. Cavan, according to folk sources, both bodies began to bleed. The parish priest thereupon declared, 'The murderer is at the funeral and he will be arrested within a week!' Sure enough, a man was arrested within a week. He was charged, tried, and convicted of murder. But instead of being hanged for his crime, he was sentenced to transportation. The storyteller said, 'I don't know how that happened unless there was some influence worked for him.'[52] This series of events was dated by him at around 1890. In a story from Meath, some local people dug up a skeleton with some flesh attached from a nearby bog. Blood from the rotting corpse squirted onto the face of a man present, and it was thus believed that he was responsible for the death.[53]

A literary testament to the antiquity of this folk belief is to be found in Shakespeare's *Richard III*. Early on in the play, Lady Anne is found grieving over the corpse of her dead father-in-law, Henry VI. Richard Gloucester then enters, and she greets him with revulsion – having good reason to suspect him, not only of the murder of her father-in-law, but also of that of her husband, Edward, prince of Wales. Gloucester stays, with the intention of wooing her. But as he attempts to do so, the corpse of Henry VI begins to bleed – causing Lady Anne to exclaim:

O gentlemen, see, see! Dead Henry's wounds
Ope their congealèd mouths and bleed afresh.–
Blush, blush, thou lump of foul deformity,
For 'tis thy presence that ex-hales this blood

51 Waldron, *Maamtrasna*, p. 117.
52 IFC Ms. Vol. 1196, p. 211.
53 IFC Ms. Vol. 1197, p. 143.

From cold and empty veins where no blood dwells.
Thy deed, inhuman and unnatural,
Provokes this deluge supernatural.
O God, which this blood mad'st, revenge his death.
O earth, which this blood drink'st, revenge his death.
Either heaven with lightning strike the murd'rer dead,
Or earth gape open wide and eat him quick
As thou dost swallow up this good king's blood,
Which his hell-governed arm hath butcherèd.[54]

A Donegal man recalled that people would attempt to place the hand of a suspect on the corpse, in order to test for guilt in this way.[55] This too is an ancient practice, as Keith Thomas points out in his treatment of superstitious practices, including trial by ordeal, in England through the later Middle Ages:

Another ... practice was that of compelling a person suspected of murder to touch the victim's corpse, on the assumption that, if he were guilty, the body would gush forth anew with blood. Contemporary scientists who believed in doctrines of sympathy and antipathy had no difficulty in accepting the validity of this procedure; and it is known to have been formally employed by judges and coroners on a number of occasions during the sixteenth and seventeenth centuries. Both Reginald Scot and Francis Bacon were prepared to believe that it worked. Its main role, however, seems to have been to deter the potential murderer from committing the otherwise perfect crime for fear of being supernaturally detected. The suspect's reluctance to undergo the ordeal might also be taken as proof of his guilt. At Ormskirk in 1636 it was urged that Joan Elderson, a suspected witch, had stayed away from the funeral of two children she was supposed to have killed, for fear that she would have been made to touch their corpses; and in Somerset in 1613 a murderer fled, rather than touch his victim's body.[56]

---

54 Shakespeare, *The tragedy of King Richard the Third*, act 1, scene 2, lines 55–67.
55 IFC Ms. Vol. 800, p. 386.
56 Thomas, *Religion and the decline of magic*, pp. 261–62. See also Ruth Richardson, *Death, dissection and the destitute* (London, 1987), pp. 15, 25; and Edwin Radford, *Encyclopaedia of superstitions* (2nd ed., London, 1961), p. 343.

While a bleeding corpse was generally an omen of guilt, in one instance, it was taken as a sign of innocence: two men were convicted of abducting a young girl, and were duly hanged in Cavan gaol. Their corpses bled from the gaol to the graveyard – a distance of some fifteen miles – and the local priest heralded this as a miracle which proved their innocence of the crime for which they had been punished; adding that, in his view, a Protestant had committed the crime, and had then bribed the girl to indict these two men.[57]

Storms could also act as omens of innocence. When a blind man was hanged for the murder of a small boy – reportedly the last hanging in Co. Cavan – there was 'a terrible storm' with 'unnatural darkness', which the local people took as a sign of his innocence (perhaps following the biblical tradition of unnatural darkness on the day of Christ's crucifixion).[58] Other omens referred to in the folklore archives include a white dove circling overhead during a hanging;[59] and blood on the door of a witness whose false testimony was responsible for the conviction and hanging of an innocent man. The blood was placed there by the man's mother, and could not be washed off – a sign of where the true guilt lay.[60]

Belief in such omens as corpses bleeding could be said to form part of the wider folk belief that 'murder will out'. It was said in relation to murder generally that 'a murderer will always come back to the scene of his crime',[61] and that when a murderer died, his eyes could not be closed.[62] In the case of Scanlon and the infamous *Cailín Bán* murder,[63] it was said that everyone knew his profession of innocence was false when on the day of his funeral, the horses pulling the hearse refused to move.[64] Mary Banim

---

57 IFC Ms. Vol. 1197, p. 83.
58 IFC Ms. Vol. 1196, p. 128; Vol. 1195, p. 467. See also Matthew, ch. 27, v. 45; Mark, ch. 15, v. 33; Luke, ch. 23, v. 44.
59 IFC Ms. Vol. 1196, p. 159.
60 IFC Ms. Vol. 257, p. 563.
61 IFC Ms. Vol. 1197, p. 60.
62 IFC Ms. Vol. 1210, p. 61.
63 See above, pp. 47–48.
64 IFC Ms. Vol. 1210, p. 52.

heard a different version of this story from a Limerick woman named Mrs Lacy, in which it was the horses carrying Scanlon from gaol to the scaffold at Gallows Green who would not move:

As I told you, my mother stood close by that bridge as the murderer of his young wife was brought in a carriage to Gallows Green, the minister sitting in the carriage beside him; an' what I'm now telling you happened as sure as I'm a living woman this day. All Limerick knows it.

Horses won't carry a lost soul over running water, nor the body, dead or alive, of a lost soul. Everyone saw it. When the horses came just there fornenst to us to the foot of the bridge they stopped, and, no more than if they were beasts of stone, no power could get them to cross the water. It was a terrible sight. The people – mad with hatred and horror of the man, but quiet an' silent, because he was in face of his doom – crowding round the carriage windows; the soldiers and police tryin' to keep them off, an' force the horses to move. The awful knowledge that fell upon the whole people because of the creatures' refusing to go, for, by that sign, they all knew that Scanlon would die without the repentance that may God send us all sinners, now and at the hour of death....

At last the minister said the prisoner must walk it, and, arm in arm, he and Scanlon crossed the bridge in sight of the multitude, and then the horses, of their own accord, moved on, quiet as lambs.[65]

Magic / witchcraft

Understandably, accusations of witchcraft rarely surfaced in the courts – the occult being notoriously difficult to prove to required legal standards. Thus, for instance, while it was believed by many that a cow's inability to give milk was usually caused by a witch 'stealing' or 'sucking' the milk from the animal, the preferred method of dealing with this was to seek the advice of a priest, rather than to issue a summons.[66] There were occasional exceptions: at petty sessions in Co. Mayo in 1843, a woman was charged with having transferred warts from her own skin to that of her neighbour's children through the magical use of a wisp of straw and a small wool bag.[67]

65 Mary Banim, *Here and there through Ireland* (Dublin, 1890), i, 240–42.
66 IFC Ms. Vol. 1196, p. 118.
67 *Connaught Ranger*, 25 October 1843.

One example of a lawsuit which was occasioned indirectly by belief in magic took place in Erris, and was recounted by Caesar Otway in 1850. It seems that one Biddy Lavelle had a toothache, and chose an arcane method of effecting a cure. She stole an ass belonging to one Terence O'Dowd in order to kiss it, believing that the toothache would pass from her to the unfortunate animal. Perhaps to lessen the pain for the ass, she fed it some whiskey. The next day, the ass was found dead, and Biddy was hauled before a magistrate's court, where she was ordered to pay 30 shillings in compensation.[68]

A strong belief in the occult phenomenon of the *changeling* had tragic consequences in March 1895, causing the death of Bridget Cleary, a twenty-six-year-old woman from the remote district of Ballyvadlea, Co. Tipperary. Shortly after her marriage, she became ill. Her husband Michael, together with a number of her cousins and neighbours, became convinced that the sick person before them was not Bridget, but a changeling – a sick fairy child, left in place of Bridget, whom the fairies had abducted. The standard remedy for this situation was believed to be fire – as soon as the changeling was brought near a fire it would reveal itself before fleeing up the chimney. Bridget would then be restored to her home by the fairy host. Angela Bourke describes the events which followed:

Her husband, Michael Cleary, assisted by several male neighbours, had touched her with a hot poker, drenched her with urine, forced her to drink concoctions of herbs in milk, and held her over the kitchen fire – asking insistently whether she was in fact Bridget Cleary or a fairy changeling.... The treatment was believed to have succeeded, but sometime after midnight on Friday, March 15, Michael flung his wife on the floor before the fire, brandished a piece of burning wood before her mouth and demanded that she say her name three times. When she failed to answer to his satisfaction he doused her with lamp oil and set her ablaze.

According to one witness, Bridget's cousin, Johanna Burke, 'the house was full of smoke and smell' and all of those present were terrified. At about 2.00a.m., Cleary asked Johanna Burke's brother,

68 Otway, *Sketches in Erris and Tyrawley*, pp. 390–98.

Patrick Kennedy, to help bury the body. They wrapped it in a sheet and carried it some quarter of a mile from the house.[69]

Michael Cleary and a number of others were brought before local magistrates and charged initially with assault occasioning actual bodily harm. When Bridget's body was discovered, the charge became one of murder. Extensive evidence was heard on the circumstances and beliefs surrounding her killing, and at the end of the hearing, all except one of the accused were sent forward for jury trial. The trial took place at Clonmel on 4 and 5 July, with Mr Justice O'Brien presiding. In the end, the accused were all found guilty of manslaughter, and sentenced to various terms of penal servitude. Michael Cleary received the longest sentence of 20 years. The case was a celebrated one, and is still recalled in Tipperary to this day.[70]

Crofton Croker recounts a similar tale, which emerged from a murder charge at Tralee assizes in July 1826:

Ann Roche, an old woman of very advanced age, was indicted for the murder of Michael Leahy, a young child, by drowning him in the Flesk. This case ... turned out to be a homicide committed under the delusion of the grossest superstition. The child, though four years old, could neither stand, walk, or speak – it was thought to be fairy-struck – and the grandmother ordered the prisoner and one of the witnesses, Mary Clifford, to bathe the child every morning in the pool of the river Flesk where the boundaries of three farms meet; they had so bathed it for three mornings running, and on the last morning the prisoner kept the child longer under the water than usual, when her companion ... said to the prisoner, 'How can you hope ever to see God after this?' to which the prisoner replied that the sin was on the grandmother and not on her. Upon cross-examination, the witness said it was not done with intent to kill the child, but to cure it – to put the fairy out of it.... Baron

---

69 Angela Bourke, 'Reading a woman's death: colonial text and oral tradition in nineteenth-century Ireland', *Feminist Studies*, xxi (1995), 553.

70 Byrne, *Witchcraft in Ireland*, pp. 56–68. The case is also referred to by Glanville Williams in 'Homicide and the supernatural', *LQR*, lxv (1949), 491. See, too, Hubert Butler's essay on the case, 'The eggman and the fairies', in his collection, *Escape from the anthill* (Mullingar, 1986), p. 93; and Carlo Gébler's novel based on it, *The cure* (London, 1994).

Pennefather said, that though it was a case of suspicion ... yet the jury would not be safe in convicting the prisoner of murder....[71]

Angela Bourke also found several accounts of child-changelings being placed on red-hot shovels, one of which was said to have taken place in South Tipperary a mere eleven years prior to the burning of Bridget Cleary.[72]

Influence

I have spoken elsewhere of the enthusiastic use of bribery and influence by the Irish peasantry in their efforts to win cases; but there are surprisingly few folk accounts of magic and superstition being used to secure victory. One tradition was that a litigant who threw sand against his opponent would win his case; a Cork tale refers to a member of the Kane family throwing Banagher sand, kept in a handkerchief, into the judge's face: 'it was like pepper they said; and the judge gave them the case.'[73] An Antrim source mentioned one man who was 'a great man for making law ... they used to say he would get the wife to hold the tail of his coat in the courthouse. They say that's why he won.'[74] It is not clear whether magic, psychology or moral support is at work here. One could say the same of a tale of two first cousins, at law with each other 'in the old days'. One day, one of them set fire to a whin-bush. He made a statement of his case to the bush, having bowed to it as he would to a judge. He then cross-examined himself on his own evidence. Once satisfied that his evidence would win the case for

---

71 T. Crofton Croker, *Researches in the south of Ireland* (Shannon, 1969), ii, p. vii. See also Connolly, *Priests and people*, pp. 101, 117–18.
72 Bourke, 'Reading a woman's death', p. 571.
73 IFC Ms. Vol. 1413, p. 384. This may be related to an O'Connell tale, recounted by Uí Ógáin, which does not involve magic:
   In another story, a device used by O'Connell in court is that of arranging for a second verdict for the one offence, resulting in the lighter sentence being imposed. In most versions of 'The Second Verdict', O'Connell advises his client to throw a handful of sand at the judge and hit him between the eyes to make him angry. This is done just as the death sentence is about to be passed. In anger, the judge attempts to pass a second sentence, and as this is seen to exceed the law, the prisoner is dismissed. *Immortal Dan*, p. 128.
74 IFC Ms. Vol. 1360, p. 156.

him – whether by magic or force of argument is not clear – he went to court, where his confidence proved justified.[75]

One case which undoubtedly involved magic was that of Mrs Shaw, well known in her locality as a witch. She became embroiled in a dispute over a right of way which eventually came on for hearing at Ballymena court, in Co. Antrim. On the morning of the hearing, her son told her that she had nothing to wear 'to law'; Mrs Shaw told him to look on a bush outside their house. The son did so, and found a cape and bonnet. Mrs Shaw wore them to court, and duly won her case. She replaced the clothes on the bush that night, and they had disappeared by the following morning.[76]

Curses

The occult power of a curse is often mentioned in folklore, but stories of curses emerging in the courts are few and far between. One such concerned a dispute between a Kerryman (who told the tale) and his neighbour, a widow. A river ran through the widow's land, whereas the man had no water source on his own land. The widow complained frequently that his cattle were trespassing on her land and drinking her water. After some time, a well was dug. The man built a drain going from the well to his land, and the widow promptly blocked it up. The man removed the blockage, and on the following Sunday, was graced by a visit from the widow herself: 'Níor dhin si aon t-saghas nídh ach an saghas seál a bhí uirrthi do chaitheamh siar dá ceann is t'acht ar a dhá glúin agus a peitícót a thógaint suas dá glúine agus díriú ar mhallachtaí agus ar eascainní orm.'[77]

Not to be outdone, the man returned each curse, word for word. The next day, the widow summonsed him to appear at Port Magee before a stipendiary magistrate named Wyse. When the widow had given evidence of her grievances, the man was asked

75 IFC Ms. Vol. 861, p. 923.
76 IFC Ms. Vol. 1413, p. 384.
77 'She did nothing but throw the kind of shawl she was wearing back from her head, and go down on her two knees, and, taking up her petticoat to her knees, started in to cursing and reviling me.' IFC Ms. Vol. 999, p. 72.

to reply, and duly said that he had no quarrel with her until she began to curse him. Wyse, the magistrate, declared that he personally gave no weight to curses; but he was prepared to ask if there was anyone present in court who would say that curses have power to inflict harm on a person. At this invitation, three or four of those present spoke out, saying that it wasn't good for anyone to be cursed by any Christian. Wyse took this popular opinion into account, and the widow was bound over to keep the peace, with the threat of a month in prison should she repeat her behaviour of the previous Sunday. It is to be noted that in Ireland, the curse of a widow was believed to be extremely potent, being exceeded in dread only by the curse of a priest.[78] The wealthy Beresford family of Waterford were said to have been cursed for seven generations by a widow whose son they caused to be hung for a trivial offence. Tradition had it that all owners of the Beresford estate since that time had died violent deaths. A widow also features in a tale from Co. Clare, said to have taken place during the Great Famine. A bailiff from Kilgalligan named Big Jack[79] found the widow's two sons searching for potatoes on his land. He tied them up in his house; and though his wife fed them, Big Jack would not let them go. Having pleaded with him to no avail, the widow went home, and 'went through all the prescribed formalities of the widow's curse'. The bailiff was immediately seized with severe pain in his side, and was forced to go to bed. The two boys escaped, and Jack died within hours.[80]

A Killarney man told a story of one Colonel Cronin, who had two bullocks stolen from him. A paid informer swore against two brothers named Healy, and the two were duly executed. After their death, it was discovered that the bullocks had not been stolen, but had drowned, accidentally, in a boghole. The Healy brothers' mother[81] cursed the colonel in the following manner: 'She went on her knees in Colonel Cronin's presence and said "You'll die by your neck too but not by a rope but a far more

---

78 For examples of priests using their power of cursing, see below, chapter 7.
79 See above, pp. 86–87.
80 IFC Ms. Vol. 1244, p. 561.
81 It is not known whether she was a widow.

agonising torture". Sometime after he developed a growth in the throat. This caused him to be unable to take food or drink so he died of hunger and thirst.'[82]

In *The book of Irish curses*, Patrick Power mentions a tale of a farmer being prosecuted for attacking a woman. In his defence, the farmer claimed that she had threatened to curse him with the stone of Kilmoon.[83] Two instances of curses being mentioned in court occur in Patrick Byrne's *Witchcraft in Ireland* – at Dungannon quarter sessions in June 1890, a farmer sued another over the sale of a cow, claiming that the animal had been 'blinked' (that is, bewitched); and an 1893 court case in Ardee mentioned a sickness curse called 'buying the sheaf', which was intended to kill its victim.[84] A folk narrative from Antrim told of a magistrate being cursed in court by a beggarman, whom he had sentenced to a month in prison for assaulting an Orangeman. The beggar correctly predicted that he would die before the month was out.[85] A Mayo folk collector was told of a curse frequently uttered against process-servers and other minor officers of law: 'Cos briste leis nó gan imtheacht follamh – May he break his leg so that he won't go home without something. That's said when a process server or a bailiff'd leave the house.'[86]

Finally, the story (mentioned earlier in the context of witnesses' behaviour in court) of the Cork woman who pretended to be dumb in the witness-box, in order that her father might win his case in a dispute over a right of way, could be seen as an example of a self-inflicted curse. Her action had the desired result in court, and her father 'got a lot of money out of it'. But when the woman subsequently married and had children, all three of them were born dumb.[87]

---

82 IFC Ms. Vol. s456, pp. 431–32.
83 Power, *The book of Irish curses*, pp. 29–30.
84 Byrne, *Witchcraft in Ireland*, p. 74. 'Buying the sheaf' involved sticking pins in a sheaf of wheat shaped to the form of a human body, whilst reciting certain incantations. The sheaf was then buried near the victim's house; as it rotted, he grew sick and eventually died.
85 IFC Ms. Vol. 1364, p. 202.
86 IFC Ms. Vol. 117, p. 111.
87 IFC Ms. Vol. 1413, p. 384. See above, p. 95. Our informant claimed to have seen the children himself.

Debtors

In rural Ireland of the eighteenth and nineteenth centuries there was a strong emphasis on the need to, as it were, 'settle all accounts' before going to meet one's Maker. In spiritual matters, this was reflected in the great importance attached to the administration of last rites and final confession immediately prior to death. In temporal matters, the settling of one's affairs gave rise to, on the one hand, a deep concern with the drawing up of wills and the assignment of property; and on the other, a common belief that the settling of one's fiscal debts was an essential prerequisite to entering the kingdom of heaven: 'I always heard that a person who owed debts that they were able to pay wouldn't be admitted to heaven';[88] 'There is no chance for anyone going to heaven who hasn't paid his debts.'[89]

In the course of my researches in the archives of the Department of Irish Folklore I found many stories of ghosts wandering the earth, unable to find eternal rest because of debts unpaid during their lifetimes.[90] The debts in issue ranged from as much as twenty pounds to a matter of a few shillings. In one case it was a pint of poitín not paid for; in another it was a meal; and in a third it was a card and spindles. In one Kerry tale the debt was owed to a priest, and in a tale from Waterford a nun was the one owed a debt. In all cases it seems the only solution was for someone (usually friends or relatives of the deceased) to pay the outstanding monies, so that the ghost might finally claim its eternal reward.

88 IFC Ms. Vol. 1196, p. 128.
89 IFC Ms. Vol. 1210, p. 67.
90 IFC Ms. Vol. 54, p. 249; Vol. 259, p. 467; Vol. 21, p. 288; Vol. 164, p. 151; Vol. 271, p. 441; Vol. 31, p. 49; Vol. 125, p. 84; Vol. 8, p. 230; Vol. 159, pp. 241, 245, 539; Vol. 146, p. 387; Vol. 407, p. 6; Vol. 256, p. 328; Vol. 32, p. 334; Vol. 27, p. 546.

CHAPTER SEVEN

The church and the law

... what existed was merely the 'laws' of arbitration and the clergy of all denominations trying to settle disputes between the people.[1]

IT IS TIME NOW to consider the role of the clergy in the preservation of law and order outside the common law system. Their influence has lasted over several centuries, and has often been noted by visitors to this country. The French chevalier de Latocnaye wrote in 1796 that 'The priests have great power over their people. They are in fact the judges of the country and settle everything connected with morals and manners'.[2] The pervading influence of the clergy in the social life of rural Irish communities was also mentioned by James Bicheno in his book, *Ireland and its economy* – written following a tour he made in 1829, which took in the southern counties of Waterford, Cork, Kerry, Clare, Limerick, Kilkenny and Tipperary, together with shorter forays to Armagh and Monaghan in the north, Sligo in the west, and a brief stay in Dublin. In the course of his analysis of 'that state of society which is the peculiarity of Ireland; and which is to be found chiefly in Munster, and in the West of the Kingdom', he stated bluntly that 'Besides being their spiritual comforters, the priests are their physicians in remote areas, and the lawyers everywhere'.[3] Regrettably, the value of his opinion is lessened by two omissions from his work. Firstly, he declines to tell us anything about himself: was his interest in matters Irish professional, or merely the enthusiasm of an amateur? Secondly and more importantly, Bicheno gives his opinion baldly, without reference to incidents or sources on which it was based.

1   IFC Ms. Vol. 1197, p. 68.
2   de Latocnaye, *A Frenchman's walk through Ireland*, p. 111.
3   Bicheno, *Ireland and its economy* (London, 1830).

The idea of the strong priest dominating the lives of his parish-ioners has continued into the twentieth century. We find it in the observations of the anthropologist John Messenger, who spent some time studying the inhabitants of a small island off the west coast of Ireland, to which he gave the false name of 'Inis Beag'. Having concentrated for a while on how disputes were resolved on the island, he found that the clergy were still wont to assert authority in 'everything connected with morals and manners' as de Latocnaye had suggested some 160 years previously. For instance:

In the absence of local police, curates sometimes have performed the functions of gardaí, and since 1960 have combated a growing rash of juvenile delinquency, which has included among other misdeeds the destruction of property outside of homes in which parties are held, petty theft, and molestation of girls from the mainland who visit during the summer.[4]

Although Messenger's work was done in the latter half of the twentieth century and so is nominally outside the purview of this book, I include his remarks for the reason that the community he was studying can, I think, truly be said to belong to an earlier era. The remoteness of the island and the inhospitable nature of the land and climate there largely prevented the societal upheavals of the twentieth century from reaching its people; accordingly, the 'Inis Beag' community could be said to form a living snapshot of the 'state of society which is the peculiarity of Ireland' referred to by Bicheno in the nineteenth century.

Priests and curates, as community leaders, were commonly called upon to act as arbitrators, as in the case of a priest at Shercock in the county of Cavan who resolved a protracted legal dispute between the Larkins and the Flanagans – a dispute which the storyteller avers had been ten to fifteen years travelling through the courts proper. Indeed, the same informant declared that there were no recognised arbitrators in his area of Cavan, and that 'in a lot of cases they [i.e. the clergy] took that upon them'.[5] Another

4   Messenger, *Inis Beag: isle of Ireland* (New York, 1969), p. 60.
5   IFC Ms. Vol. 1196, p. 53.

priest successfully intervened when members of the Lower Killinkere Fife and Drum Band 'fell out': 'Summons[es] were issued over it, but the parish priest brought about a settlement. That would be very near fifty years ago.'[6] The origin of the dispute lay in an alleged trespass on land: 'There was one member of the band took another's bog-bank, and the Termon fellows wouldn't play along with him in the band.'

Speaking in 1950, a Cavan farmer remembered 'in his young days' the then parish priest of Killinkere, Father O'Reilly, discouraging people from resorting to law, saying, 'You'll break each other with law.... Let you name a decent man of your choice and the other man name another and if they fail to agree I'll act as referee.' Parties who refused to accept the decision of such an arbitration would be boycotted.[7] The boycott was a communal sanction, expressing the will of the community that disputes be settled amicably, without recourse to the divisive action of litigation.

Some clergy seem to have been willing to take on cases on their own initiative, without waiting for the invitation of concerned parties. Such eagerness could backfire on them, for, as one man from Limerick wisely pointed out, 'People who go into disputes with a view to settle them ... are found to be caught up one way or another'.[8] The example he gave concerned a local priest named Father Rea, who was asked to settle a dispute between members of the Barry family: as a result of his intervention, 'they soon settled the dispute but fell out with Father Rea'. This happened to him again with another family engaged in a dispute over pews in the chapel.

An interesting example of abuse of the trust placed in members of the clergy by the faithful occurred in Co. Kerry, in the context of animal trespass: it leads us to a consideration of the extent to which a priest's advice and aid in secular matters was viewed as desirable. A horse belonging to a man strayed onto his neighbour's land and was shot by that neighbour, breaking its legs. Not wishing to cause enmity between himself and the man, the neighbour

6   IFC Ms. Vol. 1196, p. 415.
7   IFC Ms. Vol. 1197, p. 3.
8   IFC Ms. Vol. 1194, p. 565.

gave a sum amounting to the value of the horse to a priest and asked him to convey it to the man, without telling him who had given it to him. The priest agreed to do so, and the two neighbours remained friends. Some two years later, the neighbour casually asked the man if he had ever discovered who was responsible for shooting the horse, and if he had ever been compensated for its loss. When the man answered both questions in the negative, the neighbour began to suspect the priest of failing to obey his promise. When confronted, the priest admitted to keeping the money, but tried to persuade the neighbour that merely paying the money to a priest was enough to satisfy the demands of conscience. A young curate, however, advised the neighbour, 'Cuir idir é agus Dia go crua é díol as an gcapall'.[9]

In other words, the curate was telling the neighbour to lean heavily on the conscience of the priest by repeatedly pointing out his moral duty to pass the money on to its intended recipient. The neighbour duly applied such pressure. Regrettably, the outcome is not recorded; but we do hear that the priest cursed the curate who dared to take the neighbour's side. The tale finishes with a moral, in the form of a stern warning: 'Nach bhfuil sé ráite riamh gur mairg a thabharfadh iontaoibh le sagart.'[10]

On the surface, this seems a strange remark, given that the uniquely fervent faith of Irish Catholics was a byword amongst visitors in the nineteenth and early twentieth centuries. Among the many to note this devotion was a German, Johann Kohl, who while travelling through the country in 1844 commented: 'the Irish are the most genuine Roman Catholics in the world.'[11] Nine years earlier, Alexis de Tocqueville wrote in his Irish diary that 'there exists between the clergy and the people of this country an unbelievable union'.[12] Can the two lines of thought be reconciled? For an answer, we might turn to Donal Kerr, author of the excellent *Peel, priests and politics*, a study of church-state relations in Ireland

9 'Put it firmly between himself and God to pay for the horse.'
10 'Isn't it always said that it's bad to trust a priest.' See IFC Ms. Vol. 1003, p. 297.
11 J. Kohl, *Travels in Ireland* (London, 1844), p. 107.
12 de Tocqueville, *Journey in Ireland*, p. 42.

in the middle of the nineteenth century. Kerr begins his work with a sweeping analysis of the state of the church at all levels during the 1840s. As with Kohl and de Tocqueville, he admits that priests were held in high regard by their flock, proffering the following reasons as to why this was so: 'Apart from his highly respected celibacy, his role at mass, in the confessional, and in the administration of the last rites gave the priest a place apart in the eyes of a deeply religious people.'[13]

However, he then draws a line between the influence of a priest in spiritual matters, and the lesser power which he might exert outside of the realms of sin and death, writing that 'In matters that touched on politics and money the people were potentially and often actually independent, drawing a clear distinction between the "sacred character" of the priest and the man'. In support of this thesis, Kerr relies mainly on evidence gleaned in relation to political matters such as payment of tithes.[14]

Other commentators have seen even more extreme manifestations of this division between sacred and secular issues in social life. Blake, in *Letters from the Irish highlands*, wrote that 'The votaries of superstition, while they obey their religious mandates with slavish fear, yet speak of their persons with a want of respect almost amounting to contempt'.[15] A similar attitude survived on 'Inis Beag' over a century later, as recorded by Messenger: 'The island folk are devout Catholics, despite the fact that they are critical of their priests and hold pagan religious beliefs.'[16]

Further evidence that priests were seen as not to be trusted in certain matters comes in relation to wills. An account from Limerick states that wills were always drawn up by the schoolmaster, never the priest: 'We always heard it said that a priest's advice or aid in worldly matters is very bad....'[17] This view is not limited to that

---

13 Donal Kerr, *Peel, priests and politics: Sir Robert Peel's administration and the Roman Catholic church in Ireland, 1841–1846* (Oxford, 1982), p. 38.
14 ibid., p. 34.
15 Blake, *Letters from the Irish highlands*, p. 116.
16 John C. Messenger, 'Sex and repression in an Irish folk community', in D.S. Marshall and R.C. Suggs (ed.), *Human sexual behaviour: variations in the ethnographic spectrum* (Englewood Cliffs, New Jersey, 1972), p. 3 at p. 9.
17 IFC Ms. Vol. 1210, p. 87.

county; accounts from Cavan to the north agree that in 'modern times' priests were excluded from drawing up wills except in 'necessity' cases, when there was no other option:[18] 'The priest would draw them, but that was done away with – a priest wasn't allowed to draw a will unless in a very urgent case.'

On the other hand, a contrary view from Galway suggests that priests did indeed draw up wills 'in the olden days'.[19] This is supported by Bicheno, who wrote in 1839 that the clergy usually assumed responsibility for overseeing the distribution of a deceased's property in accordance with his or her expressed wishes:

The testamentary disposition of property is in their hands; and it is a curious fact that the wills of the common class are usually carried into effect by their authority, without the assistance of the law of the land, and oftentimes in defiance of it. In addition to this, they are very competent advisors in matters of business ...[20]

It is to be remembered that this last assertion, that priests are wise in matters of commerce, directly contradicts the view given by our Limerick man as being the popular consensus in his locality. Once again, we must note with regret that Bicheno gives no reasons or anecdotes in support of his opinions; delivering them rather in a matter-of-fact tone which does not expect dissent or even enquiry from his readership.

An informant from Co. Antrim suggests that wills were drawn 'far back' by 'anyone that had education' – including priests, schoolmasters or sea-captains. More tellingly, he adds that 'Old people didn't care to make their will until they had to. They said they could be put out [dispossessed by inheritor] if they got better.'[21] If this latter statement is true (and there is no reason to suppose it is not), then one might confidently expect priests to feature quite often in the drawing up of wills. As we shall see below, the one person a dying Irish countryman or woman wanted by their bedside above anyone else was a priest – in order to ensure that

18 IFC Ms. Vol. 1196, pp. 420, 465.
19 IFC Ms. Vol. 182, p. 650.
20 Bicheno, *Ireland and its economy*, p. 184.
21 IFC Ms. Vol. 1386, p. 244.

they did not face God without final absolution and, if possible, a last eucharist. If many old people tended to delay making a will until they knew themselves to be at death's door, the educated person most likely to be present with them at that time would be a priest.

Leaving aside the role of priests and curates as arbitrators and legal counsellors, we come now to examine instances in which they exerted a more active authority in governing the behaviour of their flocks, and to outline the various weapons at their disposal in their attempts to preserve social harmony and public morality. Clergymen in the eighteenth and nineteenth centuries had the power to punish illegal activity, based on their perceived divine appointment as keepers of the moral standards of their communities. Keenan's description of the diocesan power of a bishop during that period indicates the breadth of their influence:

The bishop governed in his own right, and not as delegate of the pope. He was the judge in the first instance on all matters dealing with faith, morals, discipline and all ecclesiastical affairs. He could make laws and impose canonical punishments like excommunication. He had a right to inquire into all matters pertaining to the Christian faith within his diocese. He could approve or prohibit preachers, censor and prohibit books. He was bound to supervise churches and sacred furnishings therein. He could give dispensations from the canon law. He could reserve to himself or named priests the right of giving absolution in the case of particular sins. [22]

An impressive list: yet in some ways, the local clergy were even more powerful. They possessed fewer ecclesiastical weapons, but their intimate personal knowledge of their flock increased the effect of such weapons as were at their disposal. Some of the inhabitants of 'Inis Beag' spoke to John Messenger concerning this priestly power and the potential for its abuse:

The informal political system is dominated by the curate, the 'headmaster' of the national school, and a self-appointed local 'king'.... The

22 Desmond Keenan, *The Catholic church in nineteenth-century* Ireland (Dublin, 1983), p. 53.

most outspoken anticlerics assert that curates have employed informers, allocated indulgences, withheld the sacraments, and placed curses ('reading the Bible at') in their efforts to regulate the secular life of Inis Beag.[23]

The local priest was even supposed to have had committed to an asylum a man who dared to challenge certain of his actions. 'The unfortunate man was released six months later, as per law, since he was not mentally ill.'[24]

The most potent church weapon at a local level was the confessional. It should be noted, however, that confession in the first half of the nineteenth century, prior to what has been called 'the devotional revolution',[25] was not a frequent event. Once a year was the canonical minimum. Men were expected to attend twice a year. S.J. Connolly says[26] that 'All the evidence ... suggests that the religious observances of pre-famine Irish Catholics were more restricted in range, and considerably less frequent, than those of their counterparts in later decades'.

Of course, any revelations received from penitents should have remained secret. But it seems that a number of priests used such knowledge in attempting to regulate the future behaviour of their parishioners. Connolly describes the sacrament of confession and repentance as

... an important, personal confrontation between priest and parishioner, with the former able to interrogate, exhort or reprimand the penitent as he saw fit. To conceal an offence in the confessional invalidated the whole process, while a person who had not received absolution could not receive the other sacraments without committing sacrilege and risked damnation in the case of sudden death. A priest ... could withhold absolution until the offender had met with any conditions he might impose regarding the performance of penance or the making of reparations for injury done to others.[27]

23 Messenger, 'Sex and repression in an Irish folk community', p. 7.
24 ibid., p. 16.
25 See E. Larkin, 'The devotional revolution in Ireland 1850–75', *Amer Hist Rev*, lxxvii (1972), 625.
26 Connolly, *Priests and people*, p. 93.
27 ibid., p. 121.

The power inherent in withholding other sacraments such as eucharist or last rites should not be underestimated. The magical, legalistic approach to religion which characterised the rural Irishman and woman of the nineteenth century meant that an extraordinary importance was attached to the granting of absolution and reception of holy communion before death. The prevailing belief was that a single stain left on one's conscience at the moment of dying would automatically ensure an eternity in hell, regardless of how good one had been until then. To 'die roarin' [for a priest]' was to rural Irish Catholics the worst fate imaginable, and a curse to be feared.

The 'Inis Beag' islanders told Messenger that, in spite of the risk to their eternal souls, many of them refused to confess sins of a certain nature or magnitude, for fear that the priest or curate might use such knowledge to humiliate them publicly:

Well aware of the power that the confessional gives the priest over their lives, islanders are outspoken in its condemnation, and many will not confess particular sins, especially those of a sexual nature, to a curate known to assign severe penances and to carry matters beyond the confessional.[28]

A particular sin that was often not confessed in the late nineteenth century was membership of an agrarian secret society – indeed, the membership oaths required by such organisations frequently stipulated that members should abstain from confession altogether.[29]

Connolly notes that confession of serious offences would usually result in a priest imposing some form of public penance – often involving physical pain or discomfort. In *Letters from the Irish highlands*, Blake relates the story of a man unfortunate enough to be suspected by the local priest of spreading a rumour concerning him. Having first 'laid a deadly curse' on the penitent, the priest then gave him his penance: 'A certain fine in money, and the penance of publicly confessing his sin ... and of crawling

28 Messenger, *Inis Beag*, p. 60.
29 Connolly, *Priests and people*, p. 123.

around the chapel three times on his bare knees, were the conditions on which the poor man afterwards obtained his pardon.'[30] In this particular case, the local population apparently believed the man to be innocent; but, innocent or guilty, the curse of the priest had such power in the minds of his congregation that taking all necessary steps to remove it took precedence over querying the justice of his accusation.

The primary aim of public penance seems to have been the ritual humiliation of the offender – the opprobrium of the community being regarded as the most effective punishment and deterrent against future offences. Hence with the above example of crawling around the chapel, the principal effect is the lowering of the penitent's personal status. Such punishments would usually be inflicted directly before, during or after Sunday mass, in order that the whole community would witness the penitent's shame. Public humiliation could also take the form of wearing some garment which symbolised a wrongdoer. A man from Baileboro in Co. Cavan talked of people being clad in sackcloth as penance – the classic biblical sign of a repentant sinner (as, for example, in the book of Jonah; where the people of Nineveh put on sackcloth as a sign to God that they were sorry for having offended Him, thereby sparing themselves the divine punishment which Jonah had prophesied).[31] An account from Carlow mentions the forced wearing of a horse's collar for a number of Sundays.[32] Other accounts speak of a *barlín* – an item of clothing to be worn, usually white, and possibly made of ramskin, though this is not clear in some stories. In 1777, the Cashel bishops drew up a series of 'Articles of General Discipline', which contained the provision that anyone involved in riots or brawls should be

punished with the utmost rigour, part of which punishment is that they shall come barefooted to the ordinary or vicar general, there to be ordered proper penance. A general penance is that they shall stand *in albis* three Sundays at the church door of the parish where they gave scandal.[33]

---

30 Blake, *Letters*, p. 121.
31 'I think that was before the last century.' IFC Ms. Vol. 1196, p. 152. And see Jonah, ch.2, vv. 5–10.
32 IFC Ms. Vol. 407, pp. 52–53.
33 Connolly, *Priests and people*, p. 123.

In albis meant draped in white sheets. Once again, it was important that the sinner should be seen wearing them by the community; two stories from Kerry relate that the *barlín* was to be worn at mass for three successive Sundays. One told of it being used for any man who 'got a girl in trouble'; the other concerned one Hallisey, who owned a shop in Mitchelstown, Co. Cork, and 'closed' three times on his creditors. The story is unusual in that it refers to the ramskin having to be sent from Dublin; in this instance, it failed to arrive in time, and Hallisey had to pay all his debts. It seems that he would have preferred the penitential option.[34] We are told that a song was subsequently written about the episode, though regrettably we are not furnished with its text. The most macabre penance prescribed comes from Kerry, where a man (guilty of some unnamed sin) was given the following unenviable task: ' ... dhá cheann duine mhairbh a thabhairt anuas agus iad a chuir istig ar fhuineog an tséipéil do gcífeadh gach duine iad.'[35]

Public penances were generally employed where some 'public scandal' had been caused by the acts of the penitents; as, for instance, by brawling, elopement, and attendance at wakes. In the eighteenth, nineteenth and even early twentieth centuries, both the church and the rural community at large placed a very high value on chastity;[36] sexual immorality of any kind was almost bound to require public atonement – as several speakers from Cork testify. One recalled the use of the *barlín* for unmarried mothers: 'Aon chailín go mbeadh páiste tabhartha aici, nó aon rud mar sin déanta as an tslí aici, chuirtí ina seasamh ar an altóir í os comhair an phobail agus bairlín [braitlín] gheal timpeall uirthi.'[37] Another

34 IFC Ms. Vol. 1313, p. 411.
35 ' ... to take up the heads [i.e. presumably skulls] of two dead people and to put them in the window of the chapel for everyone to see.' The speaker claimed to have seen them himself. IFC Ms. Vol. 935, p. 333.
36 For both sacred and secular reasons: aside from the moral aspect, illegitimate relationships could spawn confusion over succession rights and rights to land, with potentially disastrous consequences for the preservation of family property.
37 'Any girl who had an illegitimate child, or who did anything else wrong like that, she would be put standing on the altar facing the congregation with a bright *barlín* on her.' IFC Ms. Vol. 48, p. 201.

recalled a man named Seán Ó Fearghaile, a married man who spent more time with other women than with his wife and family. His wife complained to the priest, who caught up with Seán and persuaded him to repent of his ways: 'Is é an breithiúnas aithrí a chuireadh sagairt ar a leithéidí ná seasamh in airde ar chlaí agus éadach bán timpeall orthu ar aghaidh geata an tséipéil maidin Dé Domhnaigh.'[38] A third speaker remembered his mother telling him about a Father Diarmuid Ó hUlláchain, who would impose a similar penance on any boy and girl 'in trouble': 'Do chuireadh sé iachall ar an gcailín ciarsúir bán a chuir ar a ceann agus chuireadh sé iachall ar an mbuachaill a hata a chaitheamh agus seasamh ansan ag an altóir trí Domhnaí ag an Aifreann os comhair an phobail.'[39]

Further examples of scandalous activity which merited a public penance include false swearing in court,[40] drunkenness,[41] and a man who sold his wife to an army captain.[42] In Co. Carlow, during a period of nation-wide agitation over land, any anti-nationalists were deemed 'black sheep': a pen was constructed of roughly hewn branches inside the chapel door, and the 'black sheep' would be driven into it with cudgels before mass each Sunday to the tune of 'Baa, Baa Black Sheep'. When mass was over, they were 'driven' home.[43]

Perhaps the most dramatic and important public confession ever to occur in Ireland took place in the context of one of Ireland's most notorious murder cases, and is reconstructed in Jarlath Waldron's scholarly version of events: *Maamtrasna: the murders and the mystery*.[44] On 18 August 1882, five members of the family of John Joyce were brutally murdered at Maamtrasna, then in Co. Galway. Ten men were charged with the killings,

---

38 'The particular judgement that the priest would put on the likes of him would be to stand up on a bank, wrapped in white cloth, opposite the chapel gate on Sunday morning.' IFC Ms. Vol. 45, p. 324.

39 'He would demand that the girl wear a white kerchief on her head, and he would demand that the boy wear his hat, and that [both] would stand at the altar opposite the congregation for three Sundays.' IFC Ms. Vol. 809, p. 222.

40 IFC Ms. Vol. 1100, p. 194.

41 IFC Ms. Vol. 977, p. 437.

42 ibid.

43 IFC Ms. Vol. 407, pp. 52–53.

44 See also above, pp. 22–23.

among them one Tom Casey. Under pressure from Special Crown Solicitor George Bolton (the chief prosecuting official in the case), Tom Casey and another man, Anthony Philbin, were persuaded to turn informers, accusing the others. Their sworn evidence was crucial in securing the convictions of three of the accused, who were subsequently hanged: seeing their fate, the other five men changed their plea to guilty in order to escape the gallows. The case captured the attention of the nation, particularly as all those convicted (bar one Michael Joyce) had never ceased to protest their innocence, and the popular feeling was that most of them were in fact innocent. The two informers were shunned by their local communities, and it seems that Tom Casey also endured considerable haranguing from his wife, whose brother was one of those convicted. In the end, for whatever reason, Tom Casey felt the need to clear his conscience of sin, and decided to make a confession. Here let us have Father Waldron take up the story:

... sometime towards the end of July [1884], Casey presented himself for Confession at Tourmakeady Church – an event which surprised many. If Casey confessed a sin of perjury which had such catastrophic results, the priest would quite plainly inform him of the duty of restitution insofar as that could be achieved. There was in existence a Tuam diocesan statute which made perjury a 'Reserved Sin' normally reserved to the Archbishop or a delegated priest.[45] Further the priest would have had to remind the penitent that the only way even partial recompense could be made in this way was by a public Confession or by taking steps to allow for an investigation to have four innocent prisoners freed. The obvious place was the Church and the time would be when the Archbishop and priests of the Deanery would be present in the Church for the forthcoming Confirmation in early August.

On the Sunday (August 3rd) preceding the Confirmation, Fr Corbett had delivered a withering attack on all the malefactors of Tourmakeady. He said that there were persons in his parish who had committed an awful crime and who were coming to the Chapel under the protection of armed police. If they were God-fearing Christians, he expected they

---

45 Decree 14 of the Tuam Provincial Synod denounces the 'unspeakable crime of perjury'. Where the perjury was solemn (e.g. in Court), the sin was reserved to the Bishop himself. *Acta et Decreta Concilii Provincialis Tuamensis* (Dublin, 1908).

would come before Archbishop McEvilly on Thursday next and make a clean breast of things.

It would seem that Casey's wife, during the remaining days before the Archbishop's arrival, kept nagging her husband. Apparently, Casey approached the parish priest, Fr Corbett, who told him to come to the Sacristy (Vestry) before the Confirmation on the following Thursday and apprise the Archbishop of his intentions.

Anyone who knows about Maamtrasna will tell his own version of this dramatic event. According to the more popular version, after the ceremony had ended, a man walked up the Church to the altar and, with a lighted candle in his hand, told the Archbishop, priests and thronged congregation that he had perjured himself at the Maamtrasna trials, that he had brought about the death of the innocent Myles Joyce and the imprisonment of four other innocent men....[46]

Sergeant George Frayne was present to record the events in the church for the benefit of police authorities. According to his account, Casey stood at the foot of the altar while he was introduced to the congregation by the archbishop; he then admitted his perjury, and his new willingness to suffer for it. Waldron continues:

Whether Casey had a lighted candle in his hand during his Confession is not referred to by the police. But there is local tradition that he had – and that he stood, as an old man told me, 'ag geata mór an tSéipéil' – at the big (bronze) gate of the Church, serving as the opening into the Sanctuary or perhaps within the Sanctuary where no one stood in those days, apart from the priest and altar-servers. That alone would give solemnity to the event. From other sources, it appears that the Confession was not a continuous statement by Casey, but emerged by answers from him to questions put by the Archbishop or Fr Corbett.[47]

Waldron does not mention whether Casey was made to undergo any further penance; it may be that the circumstances of his public profession of guilt and sorrow was sufficient penance in and of itself.

Whatever Tom Casey's motives were, his confession had immediate and impressive effects. Within a couple of days, it was seized

46 Waldron, *Maamtrasna*, pp. 167–69.
47 ibid, p. 169.

upon by local and national newspapers. Westmeath MP Tim Harrington was persuaded to raise the matter in the house of commons – for him, the first shot in what would become a personal crusade to see justice done. Perhaps, though, the most telling legacy of Casey's confession was amongst the ordinary people of Connacht. His words, and the circumstances in which they were uttered, had the instant effect of elevating Myles Joyce to the status of folk hero: in the eyes of Irish country people, there could be no surer sign of his innocence.

The second great weapon at the disposal of the priesthood was the pulpit. Spates of theft or other crimes in the area might draw a lengthy, vituperative sermon from the altar; and it is known that some priests were not above naming persons whom they suspected of being involved. We know this principally from the efforts of the Catholic hierarchy to regulate speech from the pulpit: Keenan notes that there was at one stage a sin of 'calumnious denunciation'. The gravity of this sin was such that it was reserved to the pope for absolution.[48] Priests were generally instructed 'to avoid maledictions and abuse and not to make use of expressions which would give offence to the faithful or sound out of place on the lips of a priest'.[49]

The concern of the hierarchy, however, would suggest that many local priests and curates were less than circumspect in their preaching. A Kerryman told a story of a candle which was stolen from the local church: on the following Sunday, the priest asked for its return. It was not returned, and at Sunday's mass, the request became a threat to curse the thief or thieves, whoever they were. On the third Sunday, with the candle still not forthcoming, the priest made good his threat: 'Dhein sé salm na mallacht a léamh ón altóir air agus mhúch sé an solas agus do cailleadh an fear ina dhiaidh sin.'[50] The dead man's ghost was often seen after that, walking with a candle on its back.

---

48 Keenan, *Catholic church*, p. 68
49 Connolly, *Priests and people*, p. 125.
50 'He read the "cursing psalm" from the altar on him and he quenched the light and the man died after that.' IFC Ms. Vol. 146, p. 297. The 'light' referred to is earlier called 'solus an Domhnaigh' or 'the Sunday light', and may refer to a large candle which was lit for mass on Sundays.

In the Tipperary village of Doon, a priest pronounced 'a dreadful curse' on anyone who smoked inside the chapel gate;[51] we are not told whether the love of tobacco caused anyone to take a chance on divine mercy. Doon's folk seem to have had a typically ambiguous relationship with their clergy: on the one hand, a priest had to resort to dire supernatural threats to secure obedience in relation to a trivial matter; on the other, the women of Doon felt loyal enough to one parish priest to stone to death a process-server who served legal proceedings on him whilst in the confessional.[52]

Finally, a story from Cork tells of a man who had £300 stolen from him. He went to his local priest, telling him whom he suspected and that he intended to prosecute. Remarkably, the priest sought to dissuade him from bringing proceedings, saying that it would be no satisfaction merely to put the culprit in prison, and that anyway he might not succeed in doing so. Instead, the priest offered to curse whoever took the money.[53] We can but speculate as to his reasons: did he really believe in the power of his curse, or was he offering it as a panacea, in order to secure the dropping of a lawsuit? If the latter, was he convinced of the suspect's innocence, or did he simply feel that to go to law would prove divisive and harmful to the community at large? Perhaps he had stolen it himself: we shall never know.

Not all congregations were willing to take such denunciations and curses lying down, particularly in the half-century or so preceding the devotional revolution.[54] Witness a Donegal tale concerning a man named Ó Gallachubhair, whom the local priest suspected of stealing a cow from a neighbour. He denounced Ó Gallachubhair from the altar, and declared that if he didn't compensate the owner for his loss, the cow would 'come against him' on Judgement Day – presumably meaning that the unredeemed theft would cause his damnation, rather than that the animal herself would stand up and accuse him before God. In any event, the accused man stood up in his pew and answered the priest,

---

51 IFC Ms. Vol. 407, p. 265.
52 See also above, p. 84.
53 IFC Ms. Vol. 45, pp. 385–86.
54 See Larkin, n.25 supra.

asserting his innocence – and was subsequently vindicated, it being discovered that the cow had actually drowned by itself.[55] Moving from the north to the south of Ireland, we come across a Kerry priest who preached a strong sermon on sheep-stealing (of which there had been a spate), saying that he believed the thieves to be of local origin. A man at the back of the church stood up and rebuked the priest for maligning the good name of the parish, challenging him to either name someone directly or withdraw his remarks.[56] One instance of priestly denunciation even made it into the law reports in 1877, as *Magrath* v. *Finn*[57]. A man who had been publicly denounced by a priest brought an action for slander. The report informs us that the defamation occurred at a 'station mass',[58] and related to some alleged ' ... public, scandalous, and improper conduct ... [which] was a matter of common and public notoriety ... [and which] the parishioners were interested in having ... rebuked'. The defendant priest claimed that his actions were within the ambit of the legal defence of privilege – a claim rejected by the Court of Common Pleas:

We can see no public benefit in extending this class of cases to persons preaching a sermon and naming or plainly pointing at particular persons. The moral duty of the Defendant has been much pressed upon us, but it is admitted that the Defendant in denouncing the Plaintiff by name was violating the provisions of one of the decrees of his own church.[59]

Finally, it is worth pointing out that the pulpit was not always used to *condemn* illegality. In certain circumstances unlawful deeds might be publicly encouraged, particularly during times of political ferment. A story from Waterford tells of a tailor called

55 IFC Ms. Vol. 800, p. 363.
56 IFC Ms. Vol. 1067, p. 187.
57 (1877) IR 11 CL 152. See, too, *Trench* v. *Nolan* (1872) IR 6 Eq 464, in which Catholic clergy were accused of of using 'threats of temporal injury and spiritual punishment uttered during and after divine service' in order to persuade their parishioners to vote for a particular candidate in an impending parliamentary election.
58 Station masses were masses held in the houses of local parishioners.
59 IR 11 CL 152, 156. The decree mentioned comes from the Synod of Thurles in 1850, at which denunciations from the altar were expressly forbidden by the bishops.

Séamas – a known informer, whose denouncements led to a number of men being hanged by Ussher, the local landlord and justice. Séamas was eventually murdered by persons unknown. On the following Sunday, the local priest referred to this crime in his sermon; but far from denouncing the murder, he said that whoever was responsible would receive a blessing from God, as the murdered man had sworn against 16 people.[60]

The ultimate punishment at the disposal of the church was that of excommunication. Because of its drastic nature, this was sparingly used, even if frequently threatened. Another reason why excommunication was undesirable from the church's point of view was that it removed the sinner from the purview of the church – once excommunicated, he or she was no longer under any obligation to obey canon law, or to respect the edicts of the clergy. Of course, most ordinary people were believers, and would not relish such freedom if the cost was eternal damnation. Nonetheless, it was a risk. Perhaps this is why the church developed two levels of excommunicatory punishment – minor and major.

A minor excommunication consisted of excluding the offender from participation in the sacraments for a limited period. During that period, the rest of the faithful were forbidden to associate with him or her in any way. Disobeying this rule could itself warrant a minor excommunication. From the clergy's point of view, the real usefulness of minor as opposed to major excommunication lay in its discretionary nature. There was no definitive list of what sins merited its imposition, the length of time it could be imposed for, or of what penances were to be performed in order to have the ban lifted. As Connolly suggests, the use of such flexible measures to punish 'public' offences suggests that Irish churchmen 'continued to think in terms of a community, a unit within which people were very conscious of each other's behaviour and in which the successful maintenance of a set of rules depended on these being perceived as the generally accepted norm'.[61] To impose too drastic a punishment could lead to a general revolt and consequent

---

60 IFC Ms. Vol. 84, pp. 174–82.
61 Connolly, *Priests and people*, p. 131.

rejection of clerical standards of behaviour. The reality – at least in the eighteenth and early nineteenth centuries – was that priests and curates walked a fine line: the imposition of discipline in a public sense was strictly correlated with community notions of what was reasonable, and with the level of supernatural authority which priests were believed to command by their flocks.

CHAPTER EIGHT

Alternatives to law

The lawyer ... is concerned primarily with the legal resolution of disputes. Yet, over large areas of social life governed by law, disputes rarely occur and when they do they are often settled without recourse to institutionalised means of decision.... The character of social life is such that state law is often an irrelevance in the real structure of social controls upon which order and harmony depend.[1]

LET US IMAGINE for a moment an archetypal rural village. For generations, its people have lived and prayed, worked and died beside each other. Families have intermarried, lands have changed hands; farms have grown smaller and more fragmented. For such a society to endure, one thing is essential: compromise. Say a dispute arises between neighbours: is it more important to be proved right, or to have someone to help with the hay at harvest time? In such a close-knit community, relationship comes to be valued over justice. In this chapter I propose to look at some of the methods – formal and informal – which Irish people devised to assist in this task of resolving disputes while preserving the relationships involved.

ARBITRATION

It would appear that most dispute-settling activity took place at an informal level; parties would choose one person to hear argument and offer solutions. They would usually be chosen on the basis of their wisdom and experience, or else on the basis of their holding a position of importance within the community. If their judgment was seen to be 'sound in law and common sense', other people would be encouraged to bring them cases for resolution, and the

---

1 Cotterrell, *Sociology of law*, pp. 27–28.

arbitrator could gradually acquire a reputation. A successful, established arbitrator could in time find himself called upon not only to resolve disputes, but also in the capacity of an advisor on legal matters. Witness 'the Counsellor' Smith from Cavan,[2] or the *Dall Glic*[3] from Mayo: both were regarded as being 'well-versed in law' and were often called to advise upon 'knotty' legal problems. Such 'village lawyers' could also supplement their income by drawing up legal documents – wills, conveyances and the like. The proliferation of such amateur experts merited a caustic article in the *Irish Law Times* of 8 April 1899:

Every Solicitor and Barrister who practises at Quarter Sessions, every Registrar, Clerk of the Peace, and Judge of the County Court, and every Judge who has gone Circuit – indeed, as we may say, every person connected with the legal profession – is doubtless aware that the 'Village Lawyer' is abroad, and that there is – as his Honor Judge Shaw said, in *Wakely* v. *Sullivan* (30 Ir. L. T. & S. J. 185) – 'one, at least, of these amateur conveyancers carrying on legal business illegitimately in every division' ...

The writer illustrated the danger of unscrupulous men playing on the ignorance of their peers with the following anecdote:

A story is told of one of these 'Village Lawyers' who practised in the west of Ireland, but who has long since gone to his account, that, in addition to preparing agreements, deeds, wills, originating notices, bills of sale, processes, and other documents, he also did a good business by giving advice to clients, in respect of which he had two distinct charges – viz. 1s. and 2s. 6d. Every person who came to consult him for the first time was informed by him that he had two law books – one a *small* book, out of which he would give advice for one shilling; he did not recommend that book, as it was rather out of date, but he could give a real good advice out of the large book for two shillings and sixpence. As a rule, the half-crown was paid, and the 'advice' taken out of the large book. It turned out that the small 'law' book was an old 'Racing Calendar', and the large book a still older number of 'Thom's Directory'.[4]

---

2   IFC Ms. Vol. 1196, p. 11.
3   'The clever blind man': IFC Ms. Vol. 117, p. 35.
4   *ILT & SJ*, xxx (1899), 145.

Would-be arbitrators might use their knowledge of law (real or feigned) to persuade parties to resort to arbitration. A Donegal story tells of a poor man named McGrath who was suspected of stealing a shirt from a man named Molloy. Molloy and his brother-in-law broke into McGrath's home in an effort to find the missing shirt, but found nothing. When McGrath came home, they grabbed him and searched him, but again found nothing. Angry at this treatment, McGrath went to visit one Peter Timoney:

> So Timoney told him that he had a very good case now and that he could give them the law and that he would punish them severely. So Timoney advised him leave it to an arbitration if they would settle the case out of court. So Molloy and Timoney [i.e. *Neddy* Timoney – Molloy's brother-in-law] were only too glad to leave it to an arbitration before they would go to court. So the arbitration went on and Peter Timoney was judge there at that time.

Molloy was fined a pound; McGrath invested it in cattle, and was never poor again.[5]

Age was a useful asset to a would-be arbitrator; a number of accounts refer to old, respected men being asked to resolve disputes.[6] As one Cavan source put it: 'the man that settled a law case between two neighbours wanted to be able to command more respect than the ordinary man. The more respect he had in the county the easier it would be for him to settle a case.'[7] However, age of itself might not prove sufficient. A Limerick man called Chawke fancied himself as a settler of arguments – 'especially any household trouble' – but the village thought otherwise, and he had to put up with much ridicule from 'the lads'.[8] On the other hand, it seems that geographical contiguity was not considered important: once a man had earned the respect of the local community, it didn't matter whether he was actually from that

5   IFC Ms. Vol. 185, pp. 133–36.
6   For example, IFC Ms. Vol. 1195, p. 369; Vol. 1196, pp. 4, 402.
7   IFC Ms. Vol. 1195, p. 369.
8   IFC Ms. Vol. 1194, p. 563. Another Limerick account talks of 'old Seán Chawke' being a 'professional witness' – someone who'd swear anything you ask them to. IFC Ms. Vol. 1210, p. 12.

community or not: 'I often knew of a strange man to come three miles to settle a 'difference' between two neighbours such as a case of trespass or something like that.'[9]

Social standing or education could influence the choice of an arbitrator. A Meath man talks of the parish schoolmaster and the local blacksmith being asked to take cases, both being regarded as 'knowledgeable men'.[10] If there was no special person to call upon (and perhaps even if there was), neighbours might attempt a settlement between the parties – with varying degrees of success.[11] Other men of substance recorded as having acted as arbitrators include publicans, the richest farmer in a district, a magistrate and a judge.[12] Even the great Daniel O'Connell seems to have found time out from his legal and political careers to mete out informal justice amongst his tenants and neighbours. Prince Pückler-Muskau of Germany stayed with O'Connell during his tour of Ireland in 1828–29. Returning from a walk around O'Connell's estate at Derrynane, Co. Kerry, he happened upon the Counsellor 'holding court':

... we found O'Connell on the terrace of his castle, like a chieftain surrounded by his vassals, and by groups of the neighbouring peasantry, who came to receive his instructions, or to whom he laid down the law. This he can the more easily do being a lawyer; but nobody would dare to appeal from his decisions: O'Connell and the Pope are here equally infallible. Lawsuits therefore do not exist within his empire; and this extends not only over his own tenantry, but I believe over the whole neighbourhood.[13]

Desmond McCabe suggests that this form of 'private chamber' justice by magistrates and other legal figures was widely used, and only declined in popularity with the growth in number and reputation of petty sessions. Prior to the advent of petty sessions,

9 IFC Ms. Vol. 1195, p. 367.
10 IFC Ms. Vol. 1197, p. 108.
11 IFC Ms. Vol. 1148, p. 193.
12 IFC Ms. Vol. 1196, p. 182; Vol. 1197, p. 93; Vol. 1194, p. 561.
13 Hans Pückler-Muskau, *Tour of a German prince in the years 1828 and 1829* (London, 1832), ii, 338.

the only route to common law justice for the average smallholder was through the patronage of a magistrate. Often, rather than encouraging the action, the magistrate would offer to act as an informal arbitrator – saving the parties the expense of a court hearing, and himself the inconvenience of going to court on behalf of one or other of them.[14] Following his study of magistrates in Co. Mayo for the period 1823–50, McCabe concluded:

... one of the most consistent principles by which the magistrates were guided was, ironically, a deep-seated prejudice that a court was not the most fitting place to settle most peasant disputes. At a time when the government was declaredly trying to wean the peasantry away from the private resolution of conflict, and stamp out the 'compromise' or out-of-court settlement, magistrates at petty sessions seem to have regarded civil or criminal justice as needful only when a problem became absolutely irretrievable by all other means. It seems to have been their instinct that the tribunal of the court did not cement social relationships as it ought. In fact for this reason many cases were dismissed from the petty sessions.[15]

ARBITRATION PROCEDURES

Well-established arbitrators might evolve procedures or rules to assist them in their task, and here the arbitration process started to take on more of the elements of a court as we know it. For instance, Sean-Mhuiris Ó Conaill (a renowned landowner from Kerry) was said to employ a symbolic instrument known as the *scian cam* ('crooked knife') or *slat cam* ('crooked stick'). There are conflicting stories regarding its precise function: one account has it as part of the initiation procedure – a form of summons. The complaining party would obtain the *scian cam* from Sean-Mhuiris and 'serve' it on his adversary. The recipient would then be under an obligation to appear before Sean-Mhuiris, bearing the instrument. Another informant believed that the *scian cam* was in

---

14 Desmond McCabe, 'Magistrates, peasants, and the petty sessions courts: Mayo 1823–50', *Cathair na Mart*, v (1985), 45.
15 ibid., pp. 50–51. For further discussion of the effects of litigation on social cohesion, see above, pp. 102–05.

fact a symbol of judgement; it would be handed to the one against whom judgement was given, and that person would be obliged to keep it for a specified time. It is not clear whether the time-span was purely symbolic, or whether it related more directly to the substance of the judgement. Perhaps it was used to denote the period of time within which the offending party was ordered to remedy a wrong or desist from a continuing nuisance.

In rural areas, disputes commonly arose over the ownership of livestock. In the western province of Connacht, with many farmers using the mountainside as grazing ground for sheep, it was natural that confusion might result when flocks mingled. Though each farmer had his own special mark on his animals, rain, wind and frequent contact with gorse or bramble bushes would gradually render them unrecognisable. As an old saying put it, 'Is minic a chaill duine caora a ngeall le luach leith-phingne tharra'.[16]

Given the frequency of these disputes, one might expect a customary procedure to evolve, regulating the manner in which they were to be handled. The following account from Erris in the county of Mayo describes such a customary court:

The usual procedure was to form a special court consisting of two experienced, intelligent and reliable men who could give an unbiased verdict. Expert evidence was produced as to the age of the sheep by a skilled person on examination of the sheep's teeth. Then other witnesses sworn on a book – any old kind of book at all would do – preferably a prayer book, were examined for both sides. It must be remembered that prayer books in olden times were very rare in country places so that any kind of a book should and did suffice for the purpose. Then the decision was given and almost invariably the ruling was accepted and obeyed mutually, and the successful claimant took possession of the sheep.[17]

Another Erris account, from a man who recalled seeing such a court sitting on two occasions, puts the number of 'judges' at three, being local men 'of wisdom, skill and experience, and of course character and social standing'.[18] A further account from

16 'It's often a person lost a sheep for a hap'worth of tar.' IFC Ms. Vol. 1244, p. 344.
17 IFC Ms. Vol. 1242, p. 576.
18 IFC Ms. Vol. 1395, p. 399.

the same district states that where books were hard to come by, witnesses would swear using sacred objects (crucifixes and the like) or by 'laying one's head on the block'.[19] Unfortunately, our source does not elaborate on the exact significance of 'laying one's head on the block': what kind of block was it, and what were the consequences of perjury committed in those circumstances?

Witnesses could be called to give evidence supporting either side, and it would appear that both parties could cross-examine those giving evidence against them. None of the accounts make any mention of people being employed to plead on behalf of a party to the dispute, so it would seem that parties were expected to present their case themselves. We are told that the judgments of these courts were generally respected and obeyed. This makes sense: the judges were some of the wisest and most honourable men in the area. In addition, any possible loss that could be incurred under this system was reckoned to be far less than the cost involved in pursuing a claim through the courts. As far as the witnesses are concerned, they too seem to have held this court in high regard – not least because of the seriousness with which they viewed their oath.[20]

By way of addendum, it is worth noting that the first account also records an instance of this type of court being used for an alleged theft of geese. The woman in question swore her innocence, and was in fact acquitted. According to this account, such courts came to an end in the final decade of the nineteenth century; however, incidents of informal arbitration continued for some time.[21]

The custom of holding undivided grazing land in common was known as 'souming'. In some townlands of Co. Tyrone, the system was policed by two 'more-fathies' (moor fathaí? – moor giants, i.e., strong men, custodians), who were selected in each townland annually, by rote. It was their job to ensure that the grazing was distributed in a fair and equitable manner. For a time (up until the 1850s), it seems to have worked well. As the original makers of the agreements died off, however, the number of dis-

---

19 IFC Ms. Vol. 1340, p. 583.
20 IFC Ms. Vol. 1244, p. 344. On oaths in general see above, chapter 6.
21 IFC Ms. Vol. 1242, p. 576.

putes increased, and recourse to law became more common.[22] An example found its way into the Northern Ireland law reports as *Gingles* v. *Magill*.[23] Certain mountain lands were let to tenants on a yearly basis in twenty-two undivided shares, each equivalent to the grazing of thirty-two sheep between the months of April and November. In 1907, the tenants bought the landlord's interest in the lands. The defendant purchased one of the tenant's interests in 1922, and commenced grazing sheep during the winter, as well as in the April to November period. Wilson J criticised the defendant for this behaviour, but held that the court had no power to restrain him from disregarding the agreement. Without the protection of the law, such souming agreements were doomed to decay, foundering on individual greed and mistrust. With reference to Co. Tyrone, MacAodha writes: 'In each of the townlands visited the mere mention of the word "soum" aroused memories of "lawing" and bitter disputes.'[24]

In 1939, Henry Morris recorded an account of one Pádraig O'Byrne concerning grazing rights on a mountain near Glencolumcille, Co. Donegal. The account relates to the first half of the nineteenth century, and was received by Pádraig from his mother, who was born in 1814 and died in April 1899. Her maiden name was MacGinley. Morris wrote:

South of Glencolumcille runs east and west the giant mass of the Slieve League mountain. The grazing rights in summer on this mountain and on others to the north of the glen belonged to the inhabitants of the valley, but according to immemorial tradition, descended from the Brehon Laws, their rights to summer grazing over an unfenced mountain common was in strict proportion to the amount of land they held in this valley. To ensure this all the cattle of the glen were counted by an unofficial 'brehon' appointed for the occasion. The brehon was a senior of the MacGinleys, not, however, Pádraig's maternal grandfather. MacGinley's principal function was to see that each farmer got his fair share of the mountain grazing. This would be simple if each farmer had cattle exactly proportioned to the land he occupied in the valley. But rarely was this so. A,

---

22 Breandán MacAodha, 'Souming in the Sperrins', *Ulster Folklife*, ii (1956), 19.
23 [1926] NI 234.
24 Mac Aodha, 'Souming in the Sperrins', p. 20.

let us say, had a right to 30 cattle, but he had only 20. B had a right to only 18, but he actually possessed 28. To equalise this, the 'brehon' decided that B should give over to A four of his beasts, so that A and B now had 24 each. This is only a rough example. A certain number of sheep, calves, and even geese were equated with a definite number of cows or full grown cattle. The brehon's decision was never challenged....

The people still send their cattle to the mountain in summer, but there's no one now to see that there is any equation. The poor send what they can, and the rich eat up the grass the poor are unable to graze.[25]

This procedure seems to be more pre-emptive in nature than that described in Erris, Co. Mayo: the 'brehon' effectively lays down the law before any disputes can arise.

The pivotal role of the priest within the social structure of local communities has been well documented, and we have considered his assumption of peacekeeping responsibilities in greater detail elsewhere.[26] In the present context of quasi-legal procedures, however, I should mention two accounts from Donegal which talk of priests working hand in hand with a jury of laymen to impose and preserve law and order. One is dated by the speaker as occurring between 1740 and 1790. We are given no clues as to when the other arrangement, as described in the following passage, was in operation; it is simply said that 'Roimhe an am seo bhí stiúradh na paróiste uilig ar lámha an tsagairt paróiste annseo, agus na fir chríonna a phiocfadh sé féin thall agus abhus a chuideodh leis na cásaí beaga … a réiteach'.[27] While the above passage talks of the lay 'jury' being asked merely to deal with the routine, minor cases, the other account mentions all kinds of offences being dealt with by priest and jury in tandem – including serious offences such as burglary, theft and murder.[28]

Interestingly, it is averred that there was, in the eighteenth century, no English legal presence in Donegal save for rent

---

25 Henry Morris, 'Reliques of the brehon laws and other ancient usages in Ulster', *Béaloideas*, ix (1939), 288.
26 See above, chapter 7.
27 'Before this time the steering of the whole parish was in the hands of the parish priest here, and the wise men he would pick himself here and there who would help to settle the small cases.' IFC Ms. Vol. 800, p. 390.
28 IFC Ms. Vol. 800, p. 350.

collectors and revenue officers hunting for poteen. The jury as described consisted of twelve men chosen from the local parish. Its function was to decide on the factual guilt or innocence of the accused, whereupon the presiding priest would pronounce sentence. The storyteller further remarks that the jury were not content with a passive role, and 'went after' wrongdoers in the company of the priest: ' ... agus chuir siad deireadh leis sul mar thoisigh dlí na Sasan féin go láidir ins an áit. Chuir siad cosc agus deireadh le cuid mhór rudaí gan dóigh a bhítear a dhéanamh ins an cheantar.'[29] This activism bears a superficial similarity to the medieval, canonical concept of the inquest – where local church officials would swear in a number of trustworthy men to accuse their neighbours of any suspected immorality – and to the Frankish *inquisitio* (a group of men sworn in to ascertain the king's rights in an area, and to say whether they suspected anyone of murder, robbery or any other crime which threatened the king's peace).[30]

Disputes often occurred at fairs and markets, and this led to customary methods of resolving them. A saying from Co. Clare – 'cuirimid fé bharamhail an aonaigh é'[31] – refers to situations where a vendor and a bidder were unable to agree a price. In its loosest form, the price-fixing would be left to an agreed third party. However, another account from the same county stated that each fair town would have a particular person, known as the *maor an bhaile*, whose function it was to settle disputes arising from the purchase or sale of goods. Often, it was claimed, his intervention saved bloodshed – very probable, given that fighting was an extremely popular recreational activity at country fairs.[32]

Another frequent source of argument was the trespassing of animals onto adjoining lands – often resulting in damage to crops. To deal with such cases a procedure evolved known as the

---

29 '... and they put a stop to them before the laws of the English became strong in the area. They put a stop to a lot of things they were doing in the area.' IFC Ms. Vol. 800, p. 363.
30 See F. Pollock and F.W. Maitland, *The history of English law before the time of Edward I* (2nd ed., 2 vols., Cambridge, 1898), i, 140–43.
31 'We'll put it to the judgement of the market.'
32 IFC Ms. Vol. 41, pp. 213–14.

moladh beirte ('advice of two'). The owner of the damaged crops
would go to the owner of the offending animals and inform him of
what had happened. Together they would go and inspect the damage. A final assessment of the amount of compensation required
would then be left to two neighbours, one chosen by each party.
Whatever these two decided was binding on both parties: 'An
fhíneáil do chuirfí ar fear na foghla ní raibh aon ghabháil anonn ná
anall aige ach é dhíol mura mbeadh fonn dlí agus achrann air.'[33]
That description of the *moladh beirte* procedure comes from a Clare
man, who added this postcript as to its effectiveness:

Agus is mó damáiste mór do socraíodh air go ciúin agus go cneasta leis an
moladh beirte, agus dá dtéadh an cás céanna os comhair an dlí, deamhan
fios cá stopadh sé le costas, agus le achrann agus easaontas idir daoine
muintire, achrann ná leighisfí go bog.[34]

Another reference to the *moladh beirte* procedure occurred in the
context of a farmer selling a horse to a landlord. The horse died
within two months of the sale, and the landlord sought compensation. Both parties were content to leave it 'fé mholadh beirte'. The
landlord chose a 'gentleman' who declared that the farmer should
pay; the farmer chose a small boy, who agreed that the farmer
should pay, but suggested that he be given until the second day after
Judgement Day to do so.[35] A Galway man talked of someone called
the *measadóir*, whose job it was to assess compensation due in cases
of damage done by trespassing livestock:

Dhá ndéanfadh fear foghail ar chomharsa, dá dtigeadh beithíoch leis
isteach in do gharraí fataí no coirce, chuirfí fios air sin. Pébí céard a
mheasfadh sé sin ansin a bheadh millte, chaithfeadh fear an bheithíoch
[sin] é íoc. Bhí píosa talúna aige, fuair sé píosa talúna.[36]

33 'The man in the wrong had no option but to pay the fine imposed on him
    unless he had a desire for law and trouble.' IFC Ms. Vol. 41, p. 211.
34 'And it's much great damage was fixed quietly and kindly with the "moladh
    beirte", and if the same case had gone before the law, who knows where it
    would stop with expense, trouble and bad feelings between neighbours,
    trouble that would not easily be resolved.' IFC Ms. Vol. 41, p. 211.
35 IFC Ms. Vol. 1099, p. 300.
36 'If a man trespassed on his neighbour, if an animal of his went into your
    patch of potatoes or oats, he [the measadóir] would be called on. Whatever

In 1912, a judge of assize in Co. Kerry stated a case for the opinion of the King's Bench Division, which raised a particularly acute problem in relation to animal trespass.[37] The defendant was the owner and occupier of a forty-acre farm, which included sixteen acres of bog. The plaintiff, who owned adjoining land, held a right of turbary[38] over a small portion of the defendant's bogland. This area was not fenced off, and in 1911 some of the defendant's cattle damaged turf which the plaintiff had cut and left to dry on the bog. As Kenny J pointed out in his judgment, this was a case of two rights in the one subject-matter: the property rights of the owner in relation to the freehold, and the incorporeal rights of the neighbour in relation to turbary. Kenny J resolved the question in favour of the plaintiff, saying:

I think we can adjust the relations of the parties only be applying the test of what seems most reasonable under the circumstances, and, inasmuch as the plaintiff's whole turbary harvest, the cutting and saving of which is confined to a comparatively small portion of the year, would be imperilled if the defendant were entitled to allow his cattle to wander at large and without restraint over every portion of the bog, I am of opinion that it would be an unreasonable exercise of his rights of ownership if he were permitted to do so without making some sort of provision against injury to the plaintiff.[39]

At the outset of his judgment, Kenny J commented with surprise that there appeared to be no reported decision on the point at issue.[40] Given the amount of bogland in Ireland, with the accompanying network of turbary rights, one would expect disputes of this nature to have been common. That the issue did not previously make its way into the law reports may be an indication of the success of the *moladh beirte* and similar procedures. However, it is likely that resort to the courts in this instance accelerated the demise of such informal arbitration procedures.

he judged to have been destroyed, the owner of the animal would have to pay for it. A piece of land was what he had, he got a piece of land.' IFC Ms. Vol. 1833, pp. 88–89.
37 *Cronin* v. *Connor* [1913] 2 IR 119.
38 The right to cut and remove turf from another's land.
39 *Cronin* v. *Connor* [1913] 2 IR 119, 126.
40 ibid., p. 124.

CHAPTER NINE

A kind of conclusion

IN ATTEMPTING TO draw this work to a close, I would first say that I hope it to be not an end but a beginning. Once again, it must be emphasised that much of the evidence considered here is fragmentary, often undated, probably biased and certainly incomplete. Any observations made are thus tentative at best. If this research has succeeded, it has done so, not by providing answers, but by showing that there are more questions to be asked, and perhaps also by reminding students and teachers of law alike that law has a life beyond the textbook, beyond even the courtroom.

One of the pioneers in the movement to close the gap between the disciplines of sociology and law was Eugen Ehrlich, who in 1936 published his classic work, *Fundamental principles of the sociology of law*. In it he sought to challenge a then widespread assumption of lawyers that their perception of law and the legal system was shared by the general public. The following passage from Cotterrell provides a useful compression of Ehrlich's arguments – especially his preoccupation with what he termed 'living law' – that is, law as it operates and is perceived in reality, as opposed to theoretical law, which has no place for distortions and misunderstandings:

If we asked a traveller to describe the rules governing social life in a country he has visited, writes Ehrlich, he would tell us, for example, about marriage customs and the structure of family life and commercial practices, but he might have little to say about the rules by which law suits are decided. Lawyers tend to assume that the norms for decision legitimised by the state are the rules of conduct as well but, in reality, they are rules that, it is thought by those who make and apply them, should govern conduct. Whether they do so is an empirical question to which the answer is often unknown. The rules actually followed in social life are the real 'living law' (*lebendes recht*) which generally operates to prevent disputes and, when disputes arise, to settle them without recourse to the legal institutions of the state.[1]

The empirical question of the effect which a system of law has upon the ordinary members of the society which it purports to regulate is an important one, and Ehrlich is right in saying that it is a question which has not often been answered. Indeed, one might go so far as to suggest that a complete answer for any given society at any time is impossible. This does not negate the value of attempts to find even partial answers for particular societies at particular times – which is what I have sought to do for the rural Ireland of the eighteenth, nineteenth and early twentieth centuries. This period in Irish history has provided us with an abundance of recorded folk songs, sayings and stories; yet this rich source has been all but ignored by everyone save folklore scholars. A lack of mainstream academic interest is wholly understandable, given the problems which plague folklore as an historical source: difficulties in translation, problems in placing folk material geographically and chronologically, the mixing of truth with half-truth and legend in a seemingly indiscriminate and often undetectable fashion, and the ever-present knowledge that no matter how much folklore has been collected, it remains but a few drops in the vast ocean of unrecorded thoughts, dreams and actions which constitute our human story.

But these problems are not insurmountable; and what may seem to the legal mind to be the very defects of folklore, can, when approached with patience and humility, be turned to striking advantage, as they force us to consider stale history anew, from a different angle. We may see 'through a glass darkly', but if no clearer window possesses the same view, then it behoves us to press our faces to the glass and squint through the grime as best we can. This research rests on the truth that communities of people do adopt common beliefs, prejudices and values, and that in many instances such humble historical sources as folklore, travel literature and even works of fiction represent our best hope

1 Cotterrell, *The sociology of law*, p. 27.

in the struggle to find and define these common characteristics – the real glue that holds a society together.

What then are some of the questions which this research has raised? The first puzzle concerns the extent to which law formed part of the daily experience of ordinary Irish people. In looking for an answer, we encounter blatant contradictions between folklore and the writings of outside observers. Popular sayings, recorded in the folklore archives, recommending avoidance of law at all costs must be reconciled with the overwhelming evidence of Inglis, Thackeray and others that Irish people relished any opportunity to go to law, regardless of how trivial the cause, and were in general far more litigious than their counterparts anywhere else in Europe. Incidentally, when discussing the extent of popular recourse to law, it seems the Irish experience may be more comparable to that of other British settlements in Asia and Africa, than to anywhere on mainland Europe. The following passage from Robert Kidder is concerned with Indian attitudes to British colonial law, but it could equally be descriptive of rural Ireland during the eighteenth and nineteenth centuries:

Courts were the object of rampant abuse and manipulation. Every trick in the book is described in detail: perjury, falsification of evidence, procedural manipulation in order to stalemate opponents with delay, and bribery of court personnel.... People's cynicism about the quality of English justice was only matched by their ambivalent, gambler-like hopes for personal success. Litigants were pictured either as innocent dupes of an alien system or as conniving aggressors, grabbing for fortunes from their inexperienced opponents.[2]

A growing body of literature seeks to analyse the true effect of imposing a legal system from without on an unwilling populace. The traditional view of the conquerors speaks of the civilising influence of western legal culture being brought to bear on a backward people; the traditional view of the conquered is a straightforward tale of foreign oppression and native ignorance. But recent research in Africa, India and elsewhere shows the true relationship to be more complex. What was seldom realised by

---

2 Kidder, 'Western law in India: external law and local response', p. 160.

the colonial powers at the time was that their systems of law were often based on values and conceptions of justice which were not held by the indigenous population. Consequently, much of the behaviour which was deemed scandalous by observers from the conquering nation was perfectly acceptable to the conquered, because law was not the ultimate arbiter of justice, but rather one of a number of weapons which might be used in the ongoing struggle to maintain place and position within one's community. Scholars have begun to accept that what law meant to ordinary people often bore little relationship to what was intended by the lawgivers. Kidder writes, again with reference to India, that

Much colonial correspondence concerning the courts dealt with the 'despicable' native tendency to lie, scheme and bribe their way to court victories. Administrators took umbrage at the fact that natives treated litigation as a form of speculation and entertainment.[3]

The similarity with rural Irish attitudes is striking.

Perhaps the best and most shocking example of the use of the legal process by Irish people to achieve goals wholly unrelated to the dispensing of justice concerns prosecutions for rape. English, Irish and French writers noted the abnormally large number of rape charges during the first half of the nineteenth century, and sought to explain this in the light of the international reputation of the Irish for chastity and sexual virtue. It was suggested by most, if not all, that the answer lay in a practice of young women using such accusations to 'persuade' reluctant suitors to make an offer of marriage. This is supported by the fact that the vast majority of cases were either withdrawn after such an offer, or ended in acquittal. The vocal astonishment with which foreign observers greeted this practice contrasts starkly with the silence of folk sources on these matters.[4]

At times, folklore contains within itself seeds of paradox and contradiction. One thinks of the apparent schizophrenia in the folk

---

3 Kidder, 'Toward an integrated theory of imposed law', p. 292.
4 See above, pp. 36–37.

attitude to perjury and the breaking of oaths. On the one hand, there are outright condemnations of perjury as a heinous offence against God and man, together with assurances that perjurers were abhorred by all 'right-thinking people'. On the other, the same sources could be found admitting that lying under oath was 'as common as grass', and telling stories which admired the clever-ness of people outwitting the law and frustrating justice through lying and casuistry. More research is needed, but I would suggest that part of the explanation lies in a form of superstitious legalism which pervaded Irish peasant culture during the eighteenth and nineteenth centuries. The power which supported the oath in rural Ireland was not a respect for truth, so much as a fear of the supernatural consequences of perjury. If the wrath of God could be avoided by some trick – kissing the thumb, using half-truths – then perjury became not merely an option, but a virtual imperative. Rural Irish Christianity of that time reflected a popular belief that supernatural punishment was largely connected to specific external actions, rather than to internal thoughts and motivations. A super-ficial, act-centred concept of sin which was more redolent of magic and sorcery than of theological Christianity prevailed. This rural Irish attitude implies a significant residue of pagan belief underlying peasant Catholicism of the eighteenth and nineteenth centuries.

The contradictions which emerge from the discussion in the folklore archives of swearing and perjury are not found when we come to look at popular attitudes towards alternative methods of dispute resolution. Across the country, one finds a strikingly uniform view that arbitration, mediation, and even quasi-judicial customary courts were preferable to the creaking, expensive machinery of the common law. When arbitration and mediation procedures are talked of, one finds an inevitable contrast being drawn between their 'common sense' results and the often unjust or unsatisfactory judgments of the courts. Mediation could reach quite a sophisticated level, as accounts of a customary court from Erris, Co. Mayo prove. This court was set up to resolve disputes over ownership of livestock – a common and vital problem, as many local farmers allowed their sheep to graze indiscriminately upon the nearby mountains. Markings would become unclear over time, and animals could easily be mixed up. Folk sources recall the court still being used in the 1950s.[5] This would not be too surprising if it were true; the nature and frequency of such disputes lend themselves naturally to a procedure which offers a quick, cheap and final solution.

In discussing the resolution of disputes at any level in Ireland, little progress can be made without including the role of the clergy in Irish peasant society over the past three centuries. Simon Roberts has written advocating 'a careful review of the role in disputes played by the clergy in Christian Europe', which he says would prove an invaluable contribution to the study of disputes from an anthropological perspective.[6] Historians such as Connolly and Keenan have examined the power of the clergy to actively police social behaviour and punish wrongdoers through the use of the confessional, public penances, denunciation from the altar and the like. But there remains the question of the extent to which priests became directly involved in the settlement of disputes – whether as go-betweens, arbitrators or authoritative judges.[7] Folk sources contain examples of each. In some cases, the priest is invited to intervene; in others, he takes it upon himself to do so, with varying degrees of acceptance and success.

These are some of the topics which have been covered in this book. There is more work that can be done, in these and other areas, and it is my hope that we will see a growing use of alternative historical sources to round out what can be learned of law from court records, statute books, commentaries, histories and the like. The great Russian author Tolstoy devoted much of his novel *War and peace* to a consideration of the nature of history. It was his belief that true history was as much the sum of all the thoughts and actions of the least member of society as it was of the greatest. Towards the end of the novel, he made a passionate plea for a shifting of scholarly attention away from the supposed great men of history and toward the folk; a call to – as he put it – 'discover the laws of history'; that is, the patterns of thought and behaviour

5 See above, p. 155.
6 Roberts, 'The study of dispute: anthropological perspectives', in Bossy (ed.), *Disputes and settlements*, p. 1.
7 See above, pp. 158–59, and also chapter 7.

which have marked the human race at various points in its existence. Whether his plea will be acted upon remains to be seen, but I for one endorse its sentiment, and will end with his words:

To study the laws of history we must completely change the subject of our observation, must leave aside kings, ministers and generals, and study the common, infinitesmally small elements by which the masses are moved. No one can say in how far it is possible for man to advance in this way towards an understanding of the laws of history; but it is evident that only along that path does the possibility of discovering the laws of history lie.[8]

8 Tolstoy, *War and peace* (London, 1943), p. 911. *War and peace* was first published (in Russian) in 1866.

Index of materials relating to law in the Irish Folklore Collection

THIS IS A GUIDE to some of the topics which come under the heading of *An Dlí* in the manuscript collections housed in the Department of Irish Folklore at University College Dublin. Given the fragmentary nature of material garnered from folk sources, and the rudimentary fashion in which the collection was indexed at the time of writing of this book, I cannot claim this to be a comprehensive table: I include it in the hope that it might prove a useful starting point for anyone who wishes to explore this most fascinating of sources for themselves. The volume numbers refer to volumes in the main manuscript collection, unless prefaced with an 's', which indicates the 'schools' collection.

SUBJECT Volume	Page No.	SUBJECT Volume	Page No.
ARBITRATION		BAIL	
39	357	1196	100, 204
41	210, 213–14	1197	76
117	35	1210	13
162	114		
172	57	BAILIFFS / GRIPPERS	
185	133–36	30	231
698	377	43	66
1165	508	80	283
1194	561–65	405	81
1195	367, 467	437	376
1196	20, 180, 239, 287, 330	444	450
1197	1, 91, 116, 199	462	351
1340	583	1194	570, 582, 585
1833	88	1196	79, 186, 252

SUBJECT *Volume*	*Page No.*
DEBT / DEBTORS *(cont.)*	
1006	321
1196	128, 447
1210	67
DRINKING / DRUNKENNESS	
107	725
704	136, 145, 148
848	226
983	50
1099	93
1195	380
1196	136, 165, 448
1197	22, 232
1225	111
1361	191
FIGHTING	
27	96
41	366
536	187
733	2
998	106
1193	361
1196	118
1197	66, 195, 224
1210	5, 25, 41
1240	144
FOOLISH / FRIVOLOUS CASES	
39	298
1197	5–6, 29, 163–66
1198	352
1265	238, 392
FUGITIVES / ESCAPES FROM CUSTODY	
40	98, 142
45	376
47	405–21
90	98
FUGITIVES / ESCAPES FROM CUSTODY *(cont.)*	
433	351
462	351
505	88, 123
526	319
700	455
701	296, 307
704	136, 142
733	2, 17
848	441, 460, 463
962	567
978	256
1193	328, 331
1195	383, 478
1196	9, 228
1197	14, 139, 195, 271
GUILTY PARTY GOES FREE *(see also 'Winning in court')*	
27	146
78	101
101	621
517	430
692	555
794	471
815	169
848	226
866	326
1006	78
1147	464, 576
1167	186
1196	488
1197	182
1838	232
INFLUENCE	
33	83
257	103
627	531
643	92

SUBJECT *Volume*	*Page No.*
INFLUENCE *(cont.)*	
698	445
700	451
702	424
708	44
815	169
936	495
998	361ff.
1167	186, 581
1193	336ff.
1194	307
1196	6, 36, 114, 228, 429
1197	71
1205	132
INFORMERS	
33	83
84	178–82
257	563
265	81
266	159
700	455
821	504
866	132
964	224–29
1100	194
1148	271
1195	372, 473, 487
1196	21, 51, 147, 429
1197	14, 23, 217, 222
s390	253
s456	431
INNOCENT PERSON WRONGLY CONVICTED / HELD LIABLE	
627	335
1196	25, 413
1197	83
1839	92

SUBJECT *Volume*	*Page No.*
JUDGES / JUSTICES / MAGISTRATES	
22	482
38	276
50	258
78	101
84	178
354	271
434	115
462	347
696	75
702	154
815	169
983	50
1147	464
1193	351–61
1194	308, 544–50
1195	379, 404, 482
1196	21, 37–45, 420, 488
1197	28, 116
1210	47
JURIES	
41	366
800	350, 384
1194	562
1195	415, 419, 421
1196	1, 46, 177, 346
1197	14, 35, 123
1210	21
KIDNAPPING	
65	54
517	429
702	154
800	370
1067	187
1196	124, 413
1197	83, 180, 275
1210	58
1395	518

SUBJECT Volume	Page No.	SUBJECT Volume	Page No.
WINNING IN COURT *(cont.)*		WITNESSES *(cont.)*	
1458	360	999	55, 72
1839	41	1006	370
s848	334	1195	371
s1051	333	1196	64, 202–03
		1197	180
WITNESSES			
437	159	YEOMEN	
485	239	1195	457, 496
534	345	1196	79, 301, 475, 492
561	255	1197	57, 94, 108, 155, 195
715	146	1240	144
768	9		

Transcript of IFC MS excerpt

The following is a transcript and facsimile of IFC Ms. Vol. 1195, pp. 367–68.

COUNTY: Cavan-Meath
This information refers to the districts of Baileboro' [Baileborough], Muff and Kingscourt (Co. Cavan) and Tierworker [Teevurcher] (Co. Meath). It was recorded by me on 22nd May, 1950, from James Argue aged 88; occupation: labourer; who lives in the townland of Galbolia, and who is a native of Capponagh.
WRITER: P.J. Gaynor
ADDRESS: Baileboro', Co. Cavan

LEGAL ADMINISTRATION

Yes; the people were law-abiding. Many a time I heard a man saying: 'I never killed a man or burned a house.' That was a brag you'd hear with old men. There was another remark that was very common: 'Neither Protestant or Catholic owes me at bad feelings. I always agreed well with both.' The people weren't so fond of law as they are lately. Fifty or sixty or seventy years ago the people would nearly do anything before they'd go to law. And I often knew of people to walk two or three miles for the sake of getting somebody to settle a 'difference' between neighbours. I often knew of a strange man to come three miles to settle a 'difference' between two neighbours such [as] a case of trespass or something like that. And another thing that a lot of old people used to brag about in my young days was that they never stood at a Bench or before a magistrate in their life or before any 'limb of the law' and that a policeman never 'left his hand' on them. The most offence ever I saw committed and that was against the law – and it was a common case before the Bench of magistrates – was drunkenness. It used to be that some of the police would arrest you if you had the sign of drink on you, for they had nothing to do. They'd do that to 'make out' that they were doing their duty. I often knew cases of that kind to happen. Nearly every contrary case that came up between two neighbours would be settled – it would seldom go to the Bench (Court). Above all things, the people didn't like swearing. They avoided it as much as they could.

367

COUNTY : Cavan – Meath
This information refers to the districts of Bailieboro', Knuff and Kingscourt (Co. Cavan) and Tierworker (Co. Meath). It was recorded *by* me on 22nd May, 1950, from James Argue aged 88 ; occupation: labourer; who lives in the townland of Galbolie, and who is a native of Copponagh.
WRITER :– P. J. Gaynor
ADDRESS :– Bailieboro', Co. Cavan

LEGAL ADMINISTRATION

Yes; the people were law-abiding. Many a time I heard a man saying: "I never killed a man or burned a house". That was a brag you'd hear with old men. There was another remark that was very common: "Neither Protestant or Catholic owes me a bad feelings. I always agreed well with both". The people weren't so fond of law as they are lately." Fifty or sixty or seventy years ago the people would nearly do anything before they'd go to law. And I often knew of people to walk two or three miles for the sake of getting

9a Facsimile of page 367

368

somebody to settle a "difference" between neighbours. I often knew of a strange man to
come three miles to settle a "difference" between two neighbours such a case of trespass
or something like that. And another thing
that a lot of old people used to brag
about in my young days was that they
never stood at a Bench or before a
magistrate in their life or before any
"limb of the law" and that a policeman
never "left his hand" on them. The
most offence ever I saw committed and
that was against the law — and it
was a common case before the Bench
of magistrates — was drunkenness. It
used to be that some of the police
would arrest you if you had the
sign of drink on you, for they had
nothing to do. They'd do that to "make
out" that they were doing their
duty. I often knew cases of that kind
to happen. Nearly every contrary case
that came up between two neighbours would be settled — it would seldom go to
the Bench (Court). Above all things,
the people didn't like swearing. They
avoided it as much as they could.

9b Facsimile of page 368

James McAllister's story

NOTE: The following is an extract from 'Some of the stories of James Mc Allister of Fathom' by Charles Sloan, *Ulster Folklife*, xiii (1967), 9. I include it because, in addition to the story (a version of a well-known folk tale concerning lawyers and their clients), it contains an interesting description of the storyteller himself. The story, and others like it, are discussed in chapter 4.

I knew James McAllister and was privileged on occasion to hear him telling stories whilst seated at his fireside. He was small in stature and stooped, probably with age, for he was approaching seventy when I first knew him. He walked with a spring in his step, was light on his feet and in his old age he could still do a few steps of a jig. His face was weatherbeaten, with a mischievous twinkle in his eye, and he had a good head of grey hair as well as a medium moustache.

He wore a battered old hat at all times, even when seated at the fireside, and always carried a rough walking-stick cut from an ash tree on some mountainside. When he was seated at the fireside he turned continually on his chair, suddenly jumping to his feet and then sitting down again. He seldom kept his hands and arms still and altered the position of his hat every few moments. In all this movement the stick played the most important part of all; it became anything he wished it to be. Held at shoulder level pointing forward and the butt against his shoulder it became a gun with his finger ready on the trigger; in a moment it had become a spade and he was busy digging potatoes; laid across his shoulder it was a scythe or a shovel; or moved rapidly across his left arm, you could almost hear the music of the fiddler he was talking about. When not thus in use, the stick rested upright between his knees, but every now and again he would reach forward with it to rearrange the sods of turf on the fire.

Although not a fighting man himself James had a great admiration for any man who could use his fists, and he delighted to tell of the faction fights he had seen in days gone by. To make his description of the knockout blow clear he often needed an assistant, man or boy. This person would rise from his seat while James took off his own coat and, rolling up his sleeves, went right through the actions of his hero, giving a running commentary on what the other man should be doing, ending with the decisive blow.

A rich voice with infinite variation in tone ably expressed the different emotions. A sentence was often preceded by a sharp intake of breath. His commonest expression which he used every few moments was 'hell'th o me sowl', another way of saying 'damn me if I'm telling a lie'. Story-telling apart, his ordinary conversation was entertaining and humorous. He could hold his listener's attention even when describing the most insignificant of the day's events in Newry. It is from such snatches of everyday conversation that I remember his manner of speech rather than from his telling of traditional stories. I recall only a few of these stories, but repeating them in print conveys little of the pleasure of hearing them from his own lips....

TWO FAT GEESE FROM THE COUNTRY

These two men that lived near one another was forever falling out about a right of way: one had to go through the other's fields to get to his own. Well, this day they had the worst row of all and one says to the other, says he:

'I'm going to put a stop to this. I'm going to take you to law,' says he.

So he put his coat on and away he goes to Newry and into a lawyer's office and states his case and gives his name and the other man's name too.

'Oh,' says the lawyer, when he heard all the ins and outs of it. 'Oh,' says he, 'you have a great case there, we will win that easily.'

And he agreed to fight his case for him, so the man went away home. And the other man went to Newry too to get a lawyer and hell'th o me sowl, if he didn't go into the same lawyer's as the other man, but the first man was away be then. And he states his case and give his name and the other man's name and all the ins and outs of it and the lawyer knew it was the same case and he couldn't take it on for he couldn't fight for the both of them. So he says to the man:

'Oh,' says he, 'you have a great case there. You'll win that easy, but,' says he, 'I'm too busy and I can't take it, but I'll give you a letter to take to another lawyer, the best in Newry next to myself, and he'll fight your case for you.'

So the man takes the letter and hell'th o me sowl if he didn't go into a yard and open it to see what it said; and it said: 'I have got a hoult *(hold)* of two fat geese from the country, you pluck one and I'll pluck the other.' So devil a step did he go to the lawyer's at all but straight home and showed the letter that he got to the other man, and when that man seen it the two of them shook hands and settled the trouble between them then and there.

Padraic Ó Súilleabháin's story

NOTE: The following story can be found at IFC Ms. Vol. 866, pp. 326–28. It was collected by Proinnsias de Búrca (see ill. 12) in Ballintubber, Co. Galway, on 1 March 1943. The storyteller was Pádraic Ó Súilleabháin, a 78-year-old farmer. The Irish language version has been standardised, in accordance with the policy of the Department of Irish Folklore at UCD. The story itself is a variation on a common folk theme, in which a clever lawyer enables his guilty client to go free.

GADAIDHE CAORACH

Bhí fear insa tír fadó agus bhí an tír robáilte aige lena raibh sé á thabhairt leis de chaoirigh. Ní ceann ná péire a thógadh sé sin chor ar bith leis. Bhí an tír ag faire air amuigh gach lae [agus] oíche agus má bhí féin bhí sé ag déanamh an tsléacht insan oíche. Dúirt fear a bhí ann ansin go bhféachfadh sé fhéin oíche leis. Bhí an oíche an-bhreá. Bhí sé ina lán-gheallaigh. Níor stop sé go ndeachaidh sé isteach i gclais ghainimh a bhí i leithridh [ar leithligh] an bhóthair. Dúirt sé leis fhéin dá mbeadh sé amuigh an oíche sin gurbh é sin an bealach a ghabhfadh sé leis na caoirigh. Agus is gearr a bhí sé insa gclais ghainimh gur airigh sé an torann ag teacht. Bhí leath-scór caorach roimhe amach. Léim seisean amach ar an mbóthar chuige. 'Dá fhad dá ndeachaigh tú' ar sé, 'tá tú i ngreim faoi dheireadh.' Rith an gadaí isteach [ins] na páirceannaí [ar] an taobh eile agus thug sé dá shiúl é agus níor labhair sé. Tháinig seisean abhaile agus d'inis sé a scéal go raibh an gadaí i ngreim aige. Bhí deifir ar chuile dhuine ag déanamh suas airgid le próis a thabhairt do na tseisiún dó. Bhí dlíodóir tógtha ag an ngadaí agus dlíodóir tógtha acusan. Glaodh suas an fear seo a fuair greim ar an ngadaí. 'Ar labhair tú leis' ar sé, 'nuair a fuair tú greim ar an mbóthar air?' 'Labhair mé leis' ar sé, 'ach chomh luath agus a dúirt mé leis go raibh sé i ngreim rith sé treasna na bpáirceannaí uaim.' 'Cá bhfios duit' arsa an dlíodóir, 'cé a bhí ann nuair nár labhair tú leis? Faoi bhrí do mhiona' arsa an dlíodóir, 'cén chaoí a bhfuil tú in ann a rá gur aithnigh tú é i lár na h-oíche?' 'Faoi bhrí mo mhion' ar sé, 'go raibh an oíche chomh geal leis an lae.' 'A gcluin tú seo a thiarna bhreithimh?' arsa an dlíodóir, 'an fear atá tar éis mionnú' ar sé, 'go raibh an oíche chomh geal leis an lae. Tá sé tar éis mionna bréige a thabhairt anois' ar sé. 'Ní raibh aon oíche dá gile ariamh' ar sé, 'chomh geal leis an lae.' 'Caithfidh tú dul amach' arsa an breitheamh leis, 'tá tú tar éis mionna bréige a thabhairt.' Fuair an creámhaire cead an bhealaigh.

A SHEEP-STEALER

There was a man in the country long ago and he had the country robbed with all the sheep he was taking. It wasn't one or two sheep he was taking at that. The country was looking out for him day and night and though they were, he was making havoc at night. A man said that he would look for him one night. It was a lovely night. There was a full moon. He didn't stop until he entered a sand-pit at the side of the road. He said to himself that if he [the thief] was out that night that this was the way he would come with the sheep. He wasn't long in the pit before he heard an approaching noise. There were ten sheep out in front of him [the thief]. The man jumped out on the road towards him. 'No matter how far you go', he said, 'you are caught in the end'. The thief ran into the fields on the other side of the road and he took to his heels and he didn't speak. The man came home and told his story, that he had caught the thief. Everyone rushed to get up the money to give him a process for the [petty] sessions. The thief got a lawyer, and they got a lawyer. The man who caught the thief was called up. 'Did you speak to him', he [the thief's lawyer] said, 'when you caught him on the road?' 'I spoke to him', he said, 'but as soon as I told him he was caught he ran away from me, across the fields.' 'How do you know', said the lawyer, 'who was there when you spoke to him?' 'While under oath', said the lawyer, 'how can you say that you recognised him in the middle of the night?' 'Upon my oath', he said, 'the night was as bright as the day.' 'Did you hear that, lord justice?', said the lawyer. 'The man is after swearing', he said, 'that the night was as bright as the day. He has sworn falsely now', he said. 'No night was ever as bright as the day.' 'You will have to go outside', said the judge to the man, 'you have sworn falsely.' The rogue was allowed to go on his way.

Bibliography

BOOKS

Anon. *The Irish tourist*. London, 1837.

Arensberg, C.M. and Kimball, S.T. *Family and community in Ireland*. Cambridge, Mass., 1968.

Aubert, V. (ed.). *Sociology of law: selected readings*. London, 1969.

Ball, F.E. *The judges in Ireland, 1221–1921*. 2 vols. London, 1926.

Banim, John and Banim, Michael. *Tales by the O'Hara family*. New York, 1976. First published 1825.

Banim, Mary. *Here and there through Ireland*. 2 vols. Dublin, 1892.

Bicheno, J.E. *Ireland and its economy*. London, 1830.

Blake, M. *Letters from the Irish highlands of Connemara by a family party*. London, 1825.

Breathnach, R. *The man from Cape Clear*. Dublin, 1975. First published in Irish, 1940.

Brewer, J. and Styles, J. (ed.). *An ungovernable people: the English and their law in the 17th and 18th centuries*. London, 1980.

Brown, Terence. *Ireland, a social and cultural history 1922–1979*. London, 1981.

Buckley, A. and Anderson, K. *Brotherhoods in Ireland*. Ulster Folk and Transport Museum, Cultra, Co. Down, 1988.

Butler, Hubert. *Escape from the anthill*. Mullingar, 1986.

Byrne, P. *Witchcraft in Ireland*. Cork, 1975.

Carleton, William. *Traits and stories of the Irish peasantry*. 1st series, 2 vols. New York, 1979. First published 1830.

— *Traits and stories of the Irish peasantry*. 2nd series, 3 vols. New York, 1979. First published 1832.

— *Traits and stories of the Irish peasantry*. New ed. 2 vols. Dublin, 1844.

— *Autobiography*. New York, 1979. First published 1896.

— *The black prophet*. New York, 1979. First published 1847.

— *Valentine McClutchy*. New York, 1979. First published 1845.

Carr, John. *The stranger in Ireland*. London, 1806.

Comyn, James. *Irish at law: a selection of famous and unusual cases*. London, 1981.

Connery, D.S. *The Irish*. London, 1972.

Connolly, S.J. *Priests and people in pre-famine Ireland, 1780–1845.* Dublin, 1982.

Corkery, Daniel. *The hidden Ireland: a study of Gaelic Munster in the 18th century.* 2nd ed. Dublin, 1925.

Cotterrell, R. *The sociology of law: an introduction.* 2nd ed. London, 1992.

Croker, Thomas Crofton. *Researches in the south of Ireland.* Shannon, 1969. First published 1824.

Curran, William H. *Sketches of the Irish bar.* London, 1855.

Curwen, J.C. *Observations on the state of Ireland.* 2 vols. London, 1818.

Delany, V.T.H. *Christopher Palles.* Dublin, 1966.

Dillon, Myles. *There was a king in Ireland.* Austin, Texas, 1971.

Dorson, Richard M. *Folklore and Fakelore.* Cambridge, Mass., 1976.

Dundes, Alan. *Interpreting folklore.* Bloomington, Indiana, 1980.

— *The study of folklore.* Englewood Cliffs, New Jersey, 1965.

Dworkin, Ronald. *Law's empire.* Cambridge, Mass., 1986.

Ehrlich, Eugen. *Fundamental principles of the sociology of law.* Cambridge, Mass., 1936.

Evans, G.E. *Where beards wag all: the relevance of the oral tradition.* London, 1970.

Foster, Roy F. *Modern Ireland, 1600–1972.* London, 1989.

Galanter, Marc (ed.). *Law and society in modern India.* Oxford, 1989.

Gébler, Carlo. *The cure.* London, 1994.

Glassford, J. *Notes of three tours in Ireland, in 1824 and 1826.* Bristol, 1832.

Griffin, Gerald. *The collegians.* New York, 1979. First published 1829.

— *Tracy's ambition.* New York, 1979. First published 1829.

— *Tales of the Munster festivals.* New York, 1979. First published 1827.

— *Holland-tide.* New York, 1979. First published 1827.

Grousset, Paschal. *Ireland's disease: the English in Ireland, 1887.* Belfast, 1986.

Hall, J. *Tour through Ireland.* 2 vols. London, 1813.

Hardiman, J. *A history of the town and county of the town of Galway from the earliest period to the present time.* Dublin, 1820.

Harrington, John P. (ed.). *The English traveller in Ireland: accounts of Ireland and the Irish through 5 centuries.* Dublin, 1991.

Hay, Douglas. (ed.). *Albion's fatal tree: crime and society in 18th century England.* London, 1975.

Healy, Maurice. *The old Munster circuit.* Cork, 1979. First published 1939.

Hoebel, E.A. *The law of primitive man.* Cambridge, Mass., 1954.

— *The Cheyennes: Indians of the great plains.* 2nd ed. New York, 1978.

Holmes, G. *Sketches of some of the southern counties of Ireland, collected during a tour in the autumn of 1797.* Whitegate, Co. Clare, 1987.

Inglis, Henry D. *Ireland in 1834.* 2 vols. London, 1835.

Johnson, J. *A tour in Ireland.* London, 1844.

Keenan, Desmond J. *The Catholic church in 19th century Ireland: a sociological study.* Dublin, 1983.

Kelsen, Hans. *General theory of law and state.* Cambridge, Mass., 1949.

Kennedy, P. *Legends of Mt. Leinster.* Dublin, 1855.

Kerr, Donal A. *Peel, priests and politics: Sir Robert Peel's administration and the Roman Catholic church in Ireland, 1841–1846.* Oxford, 1982.

Kohl, J.G. *Travels in Ireland.* London, 1844.

Kotsonouris, Mary. *Retreat from revolution: the Dáil courts, 1920–24.* Dublin, 1994.

Krappe, A. *The science of folklore.* London, 1962.

Latocnaye, le chevalier de. *A Frenchman's walk through Ireland, 1796–1797.* Belfast, 1984. First published (in French) 1797, (in English) 1917.

Mann, K. *Law in colonial Africa.* London, 1991.

McDowell, R.B. *Ireland in the age of imperialism and revolution, 1760–1801.* Oxford, 1979.

Messenger, John C. *Inis Beag: isle of Ireland.* New York, 1969.

Ó Catháin, Séamas. *Irish life and lore.* Dublin, 1982.

O'Connell, Maurice (ed.). *The correspondence of Daniel O'Connell.* 8 vols. Dublin, 1972–80.

Ó Faoláin, Seán. *The Irish.* West Drayton, 1947.

O'Farrell, P. *Superstitions of the Irish country people.* Dublin, 1982.

O'Higgins, Paul. *A bibliography of Irish trials and other legal proceedings.* Abingdon, 1986.

Orel, H. *Irish history and culture: aspects of a people's heritage.* Dublin, 1979.

Ó Riain, Dónal and Ó Cinnéide, Séamas. *The history and folklore of Parteen and Meelick.* Limerick, 1991.

Osborough, W.N. (ed.). *The Irish Legal History Society.* Dublin, 1989.

— and Hogan, D. (ed.). *Brehons, serjeants and attorneys: studies in the history of the Irish legal profession.* Dublin, 1990.

Ó Súilleabháin, Seán. *Irish folk custom and belief.* Dublin, 1977.

— *A handbook of Irish folklore.* Dublin, 1942.

Otway, Caesar. *Sketches in Ireland.* Dublin, 1827.

— *Sketches in Erris and Tyrawley.* Dublin, 1850.

Plumpton, A. *Narrative of a residence in Ireland.* London, 1815.

Pollock, F. and Maitland, F.W. *The history of English law before the time of Edward I.* 2nd ed. 2 vols., Cambridge, 1898.

Power, P. *The book of Irish curses.* Dublin, 1974.

Prest, William R. *The rise of the barristers: a social history of the English bar, 1590–1640.* Oxford, 1991.

Pritt, D.N. *Law in the colonies*. London, 1971.

Pückler-Muskau, Hans. *Tour of a German prince in the years 1828 and 1829*. 2 vols. London, 1832.

Radford, Edwin. *Encyclopaedia of superstitions*. 2nd ed., London, 1961.

Reid, Thomas. *Travels in Ireland in the year 1822*. London, 1823.

Richardson, Ruth. *Death, dissection and the destitute*. London, 1987.

Schauer, F. *Playing by the rules*. Oxford, 1991.

Shapiro, M. *Courts: a comparative and political analysis*. Chicago, 1981.

Sheehan, Canon Patrick. *Glenanaar*. Dublin, 1989. First published 1905.

Sheehan, T. *Excursions from Bandon, in the south of Ireland, by a plain Englishman*. London, 1825.

Shklar, Judith. *Legalism*. Cambridge, Mass., 1971.

Sloan, B. *The pioneers of Anglo-Irish fiction, 1800–1850*. New York, 1986.

Somerville, E. and Ross, M. *The complete experiences of an Irish R.M.* London, 1970. First published 1928.

Stein, P. and Shand, J. *Legal values in western society*. Edinburgh, 1974.

Synge, John Millington. *The Aran islands*. Oxford, 1979. First published 1907.

Thackeray, William Makepeace. *The Irish sketchbook, 1842*. Belfast, 1985.

Therman, D.H. *Stories from Tory island*. Dublin, 1989.

Thomas, Keith. *Religion and the decline of magic*. London, 1973.

Thompson, Stith. *Motif-index of folk literature*. Bloomington, Indiana, 1955.

Tocqueville, Alexis de. *Journey in Ireland, July–August 1835*. Dublin, 1990.

Tolstoy, Leo. *War and peace*. London, 1943. First published in Russian, 1866.

Trench, Charles. *The great Dan: a biography of Daniel O'Connell*. London, 1984.

Uí Ógáin, Ríonach. *An rí gan choróin: Dónall Ó Conaill sa bhéaloideas*. Dublin, 1984.

— *Immortal Dan: Daniel O'Connell in Irish folk tradition*. Dublin, 1995.

Uris, Leon. *Trinity*. London, 1976.

Vansina, Jan. *Oral tradition – a study in historical methodology*. London, 1965.

Waldron, Jarlath. *Maamtrasna: the murders and the mystery*. Dublin, 1992.

Walker, Brian M. *Sentry Hill: an Ulster farm and family*. Belfast, 1981.

Wall, Maureen. *Catholic Ireland in the 18th century*. Dublin, 1989.

Walsh, J.E. *Rakes and ruffians: the underworld of Georgian Dublin*. Dublin, 1979. First published 1847 as *Ireland 60 years ago*.

White, Terence de Vere. *The road of excess*. Dublin, 1946.

Wilde, Sir William. *Irish popular superstitions*. Dublin, 1972. First published 1852.

Yeats, William Butler. *Representative Irish tales.* London, 1979. First published 1891.

Young, A. *A tour in Ireland,* ed. Constantia Maxwell. Belfast, 1983. *A tour* first published 1779.

Zola, Emile. *La terre (The earth).* London, 1980. First published in French, 1887.

ARTICLES

Anon. 'Village lawyers.' *ILT & SJ,* xxxiii (1899), 145.

— 'Choice anecdotes of Irish bench and bar.' *ILT & SJ,* xxxi (1897), 296.

Bell, Christine. 'Alternative justice in Ireland.' In Dawson, N., Greer, D. and Ingram, P. (ed.). *One hundred and fifty years of Irish law.* Belfast, 1996.

Carleton, William. 'O'Sullivan's love: a legend of Edenmore.' *Dublin University Magazine,* xxix (1847), 277.

Casey, D.J. 'Wildgoose Lodge: the evidence and the lore.' *Louth Arch Soc J,* xviii (1956), 140.

Curtin, Chris. 'Social order, interpersonal relations and disputes in a west of Ireland community.' In Tomlinson, M. & ors. (ed.). *Whose law and order? Aspects of crime and social control in Irish society.* Belfast, 1988.

Dawson, Norma. 'Illicit distillation and the revenue police in Ireland.' *Ir Jur,* xii (1977), 282.

Dowling, A. 'A parliamentary history of the law of distress for rent from 1845.' In Dawson, N., Greer, D. and Ingram, P. (ed.). *One hundred and fifty years of Irish law.* Belfast, 1996.

Geary, R. and Morison, J. 'An illustration of the literary approach to the study of law: the "mysteries" novels of the 19th century and the "Troubles thriller".' In Dawson, N., Greer, D. and Ingram, P. (ed.). *One hundred and fifty years of Irish law.* Belfast, 1996.

Larkin, E. 'The devotional revolution in Ireland 1850–75'. *Amer Hist Rev,* lxxvii (1972), 625.

Kidder, Robert L. 'Western law in India: external law and local response.' In Johnson, H. (ed.), *Social system and legal process.* San Francisco, 1978.

— 'Toward an integrated theory of imposed law.' In Burman, S. and Harrell-Bond, B.E., (ed.). *The imposition of law.* New York, 1979.

MacAodha, Breandán. 'Souming in the Sperrins.' *Ulster Folklife,* ii (1956), 19.

MacCabe, D. 'Magistrates, peasants, and the petty sessions courts: Mayo 1823–50.' *Cathair na Mart*, v (1985), 45.

MacGréine, Pádraig. 'Some notes on tinkers and their cant.' *Béaloideas*, iv (1933–34), 260.

McDowell, R.B. 'The Irish courts of law, 1801–1914.' *IHS*, x (1957), 363.

Messenger, John C. 'Sex and repression in an Irish folk community.' In Marshall, D.S. and Suggs, R.C. (ed.). *Human sexual behaviour: variations in the ethnographic spectrum*. Englewood Cliffs, New Jersey, 1972.

Morris, Henry. 'Reliques of the brehon laws and other ancient usages in Ulster.' *Béaloideas*, ix (1939), 288.

Ó Muirí, Réamonn. 'The burning of Wildgoose Lodge: a selection of documents.' *Louth Arch Soc J*, xxi (1986), 117.

Osborough, W.N. 'The Irish legal system, 1796–1877.' In Costello, C. (ed.). *The Four Courts: 200 years*. Dublin, 1996.

Paterson, T.F.G. 'The burning of Wildgoose Lodge.' *Louth Arch Soc J*, xii (1950), 159.

Roberts, Simon. 'The study of dispute: anthropological perspec-tives.' In Bossy, J. (ed.), *Disputes and settlements: law and human relations in the West*. Cambridge, 1983.

Sloan, C. 'Some of the stories of James McAllister.' *Ulster Folklife*, xiii (1967), 9.

Tillhagen, C. 'Reality and folklore research.' In Almquist, Bo and ors. (ed.). *Hereditas*. Dublin, 1975.

Index

The Irish Legal History Society

Established in 1988 to encourage the study and advance the knowledge of the history of Irish law, especially by the publication of original documents and of works relating to the history of Irish law, including its institutions, doctrines and personalities, and the reprinting or editing of works of sufficient rarity or importance.

PATRONS

The Hon. Mr Justice
Liam Hamilton

Rt. Hon. Sir Robert Carswell

LIFE MEMBERS

The Hon.
T.A. Finlay

Rt. Hon.
Lord Hutton

COUNCIL, 1996

PRESIDENT
Daire Hogan, esq.

VICE-PRESIDENTS

Professor D.S. Greer

J.I. Mc Guire, esq.

SECRETARIES
Professor W.N. Osborough
Dr. A. Dowling

TREASURERS
R.D. Marshall esq.
J. Leckey, esq.

ORDINARY MEMBERS

The Hon. Mr Justice Costello

Professor G.J. Hand

J.F. Larkin, esq.

J.A.L. McLean, esq., Q.C.

R. O'Hanlon, esq.

His Honour Judge Hart, Q.C.
(co-opted)